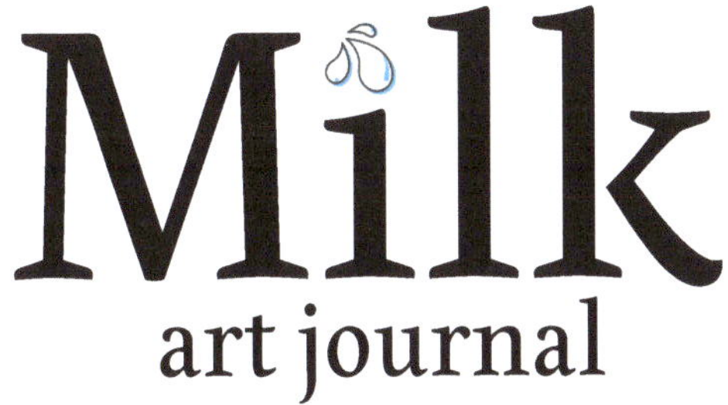
Milk
art journal

Works by
Artist-Mothers
about Motherhood

Edited by Katherine Oktober Matthews

Vol. 1
Chores & Transcendence

Vol. 2
Body & Belonging

Vol. 3
Purpose & Ambivalence

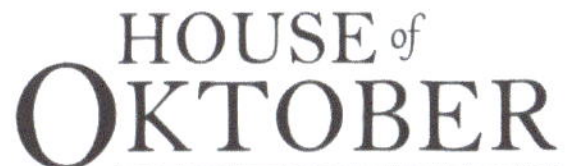
HOUSE *of*
OKTOBER

HOUSE of OKTOBER

House of Oktober is an independent arts publisher based in The Netherlands.

houseofoktober.com

Milk Art Journal
Volume 1, Chores & Transcendence

Editor: Matthews, Katherine Oktober

Subjects: Art; Motherhood; Artist-Mothers; Women in Art; Writing; Visual Arts; Interviews; Biography.

ISBN 9789493075023

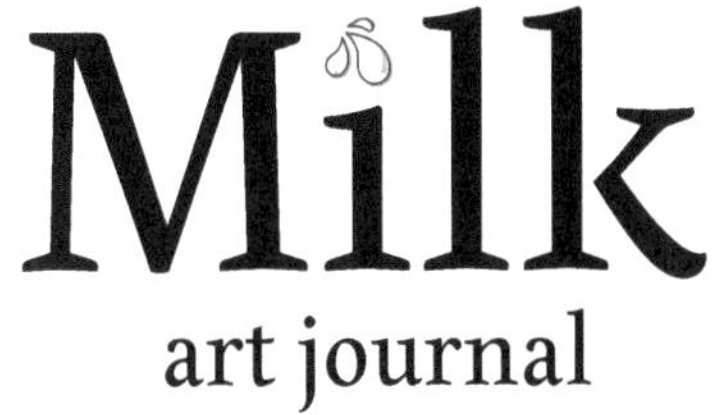

Milk

art journal

Vol. 1
Chores & Transcendence

Works by Artist-Mothers about Motherhood

Edited by
Katherine Oktober Matthews

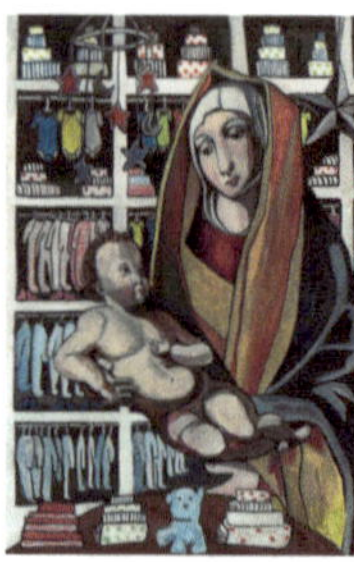

About the cover art:

Mary's Torments of the Passion (NW3)
(2022) by Sarah Lightman.
Watercolor on paper, 297 x 420 mm.

See her series *Biblical Domestic*
on page 104.

Table of Contents

To make life is the original and ultimate act of creation – a fact that has long been undermined by the myth of 'the creative genius.' It is, after all, physical rather than intellectual, biological rather than cultural. It is 'women's work,' a classic euphemism for lesser work.

Maybe it's just because mothering isn't blinked into being, it's messy. There are sticky fingers and sticky floors. There's vomit that needs cleaning up. There's laundry and diapers. The labor of mothering is less glamorous than some archetypical creator alone at a desk, communing with the divine through art and mind. Yet, buried among those heaps of laundry, hidden between diaper pails and baby wipes, there are moments of awe. Private smiles, secret jokes, first steps.

Yet, what are we to make of artist-mothers, who manage to create both life and works of art? With all those demands of child and house, with bottomless to-do lists compounded by real world concerns like paying bills and keeping safe in a world riddled with war, pandemics and the effects of climate change, is there still room to make art? Let's ignore all the bullshit 'shoulds' surrounding a mother's role and what her priorities 'ought' to be, and just consider: does that leave any time or headspace for the mental abstractions of art? Given the constant radio chatter of children and their infinite needs, how can a person possibly manage to hear and heed the voice inside?

It is nothing short of a miracle that artist-mothers exist and yet it is so obvious that they must: They are the acme of creation.

Chores & Transcendence

In putting this journal together with the artists, our efforts have been constantly interrupted: By sick children in need of tending, by sibling arguments overflowing into a video chat, by naptimes that are over all too soon, by the mundane urgencies of domestic life, by work responsibilities, or by our multi-threaded artist-mother minds struggling to keep up with ambitions.

More than that, the time often felt *stolen*. As editor, I feel a responsibility for that time: Every minute that one of these artist-mothers spent with me was a minute away from their children. It was a minute that I was not with my child.

The time you spend turning through these pages is stolen, too.

But there's our old companion, maternal guilt, keeping us in our place. Just another chore to be transcended.

Katherine Oktober Matthews
Editor

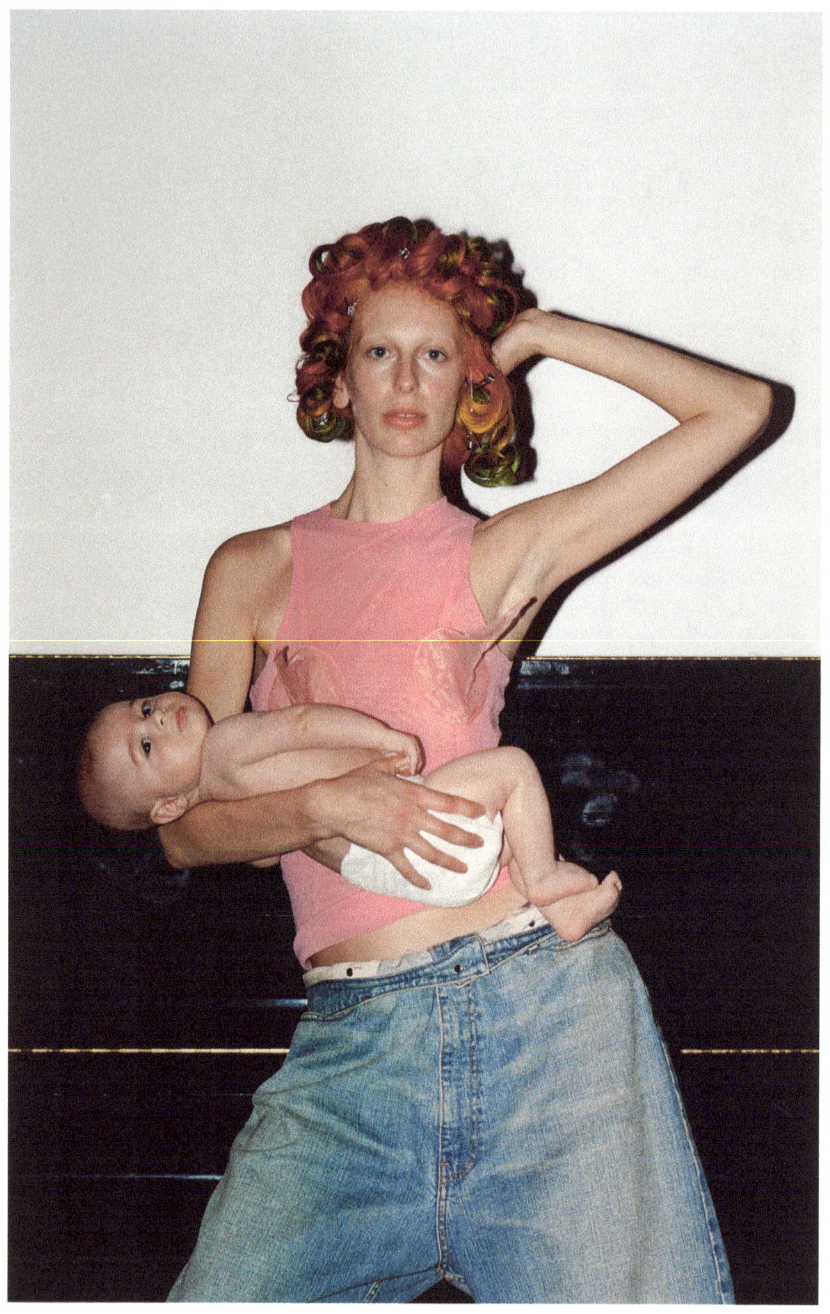

Talia Chetrit, 'Baby Model, 2020/2022.', from JOKE (MACK, 2022).
Courtesy of the artist and MACK.

Talia **Chetrit**

b. 1982 USA

JOKE

Talia Chetrit brings together a mixture of family photos, street photography, still lifes, self-portraits and images from her personal archive to create *JOKE*, a book that takes its sense of humor seriously.

Oscillating wildly between scenes of style and sloppiness, clutter and order, sex appeal and ambiguity, Chetrit creates a whirlwind of pleasurable chaos. She toys with gender roles and family life, as well as the absurdity of domesticity. While the images are shot with a directness that feels like something raw cutting through the artifice of formality, reality is still obfuscated through heavy layers of irony and comedy. Chetrit interweaves the everyday with the unexpected to create photographs are equal parts joy and confusion—perhaps like life itself.

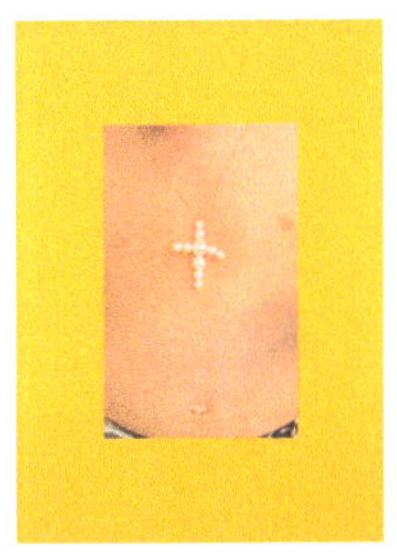

Hardback
128 pages
24 x 31.5 cm
MACK, Sept. 2022
ISBN 978-1-913620-72-1
€45 / £35 / $55

mackbooks.co.uk

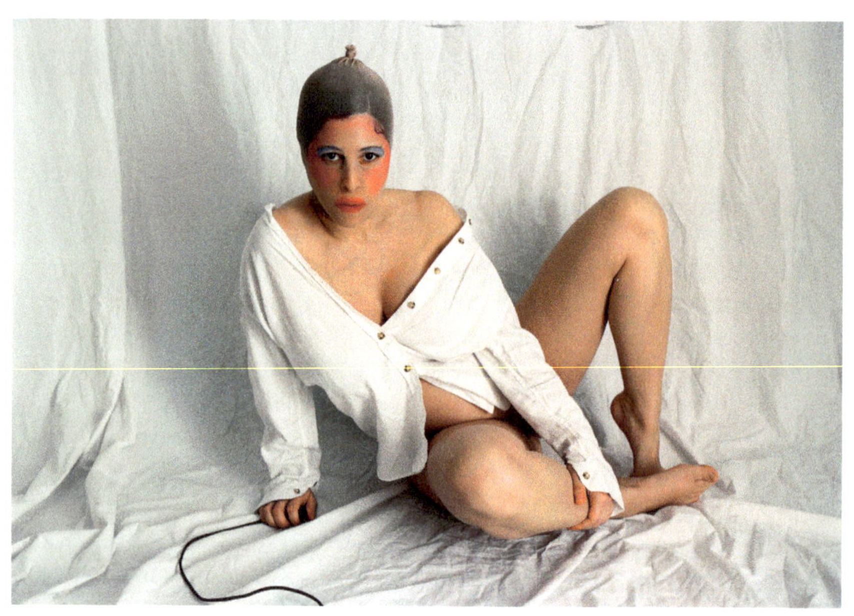

Talia Chetrit, 'Pregnant (Corey Tippin Make-up #1), 2021.', from JOKE
(MACK, 2022). Courtesy of the artist and MACK.

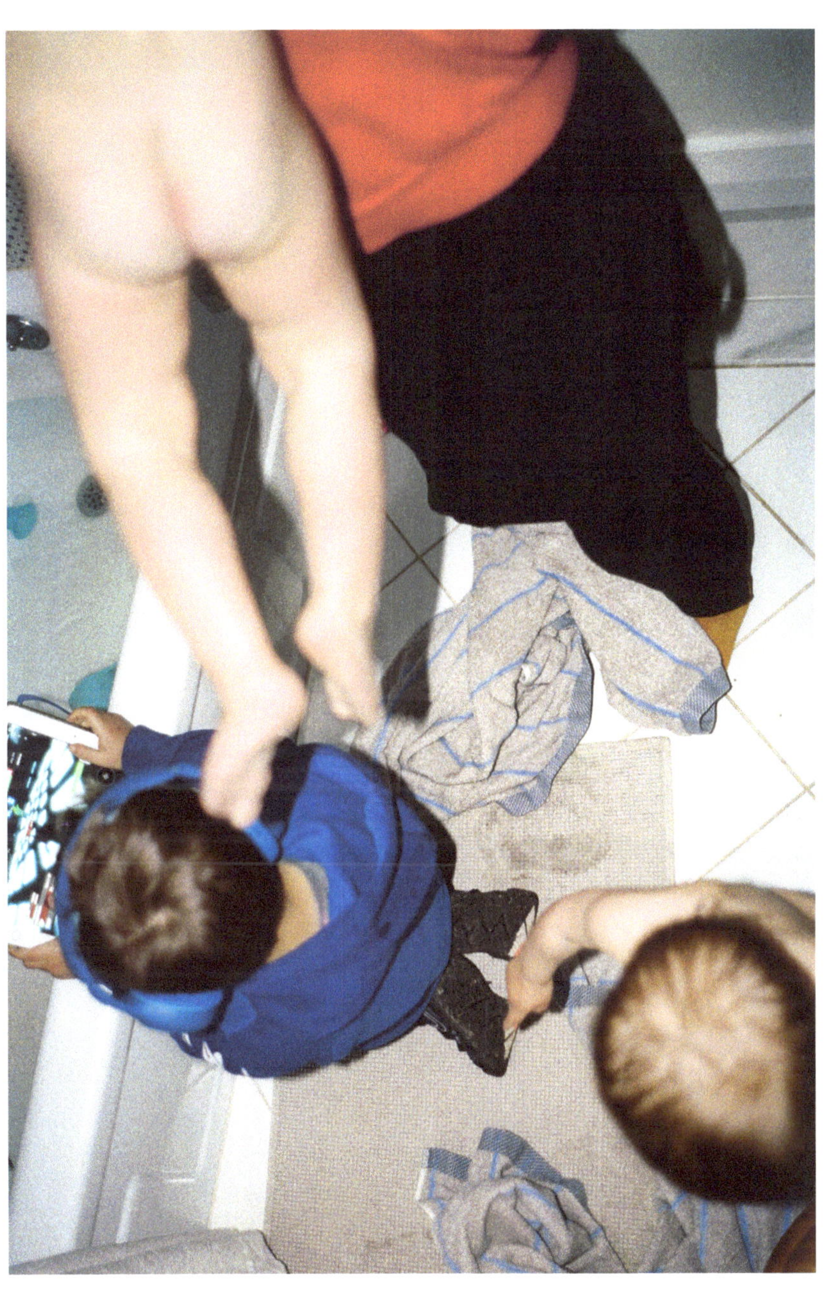

Talia Chetrit, 'Bathroom, 2021.', from JOKE (MACK, 2022).
Courtesy of the artist and MACK.

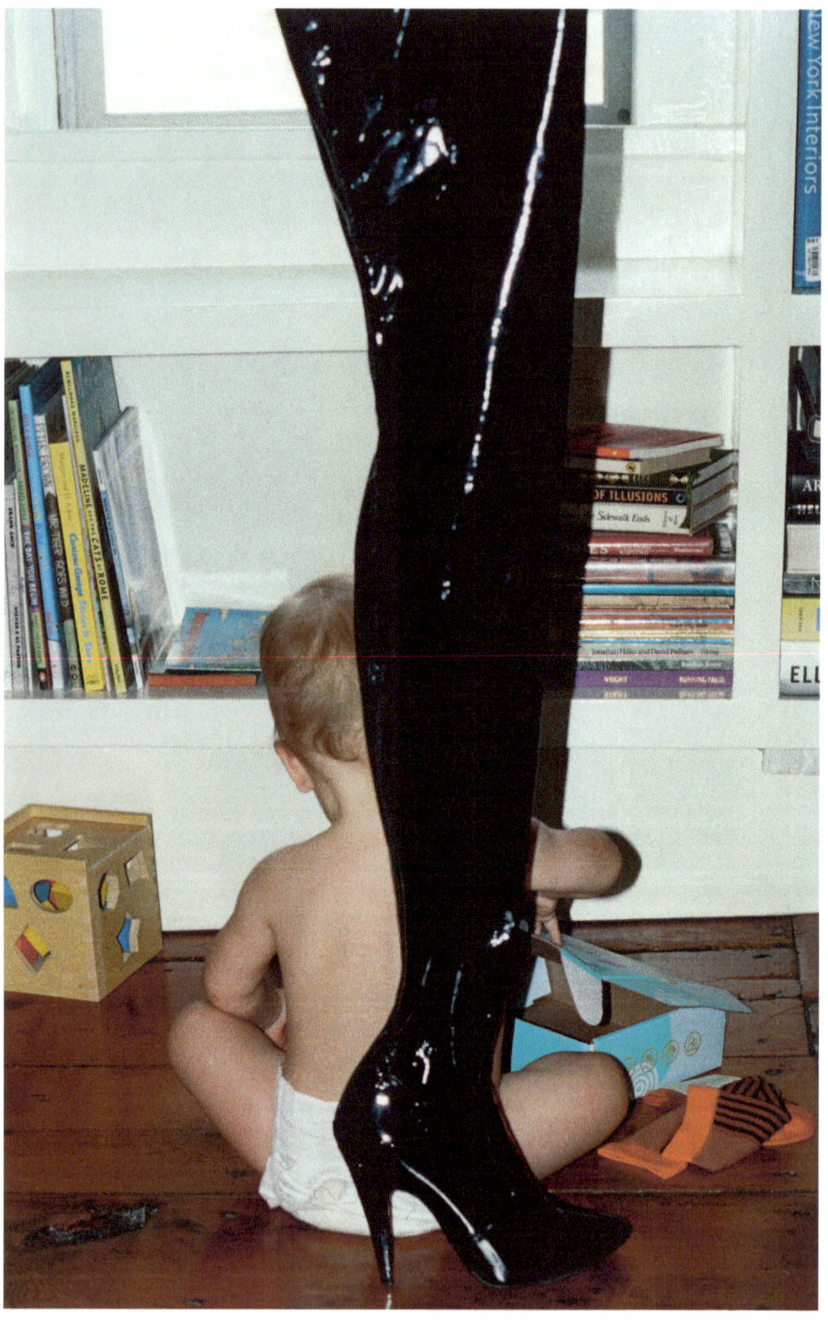

Talia Chetrit, 'Boot/Baby, 2020.', from JOKE (MACK, 2022).
Courtesy of the artist and MACK.

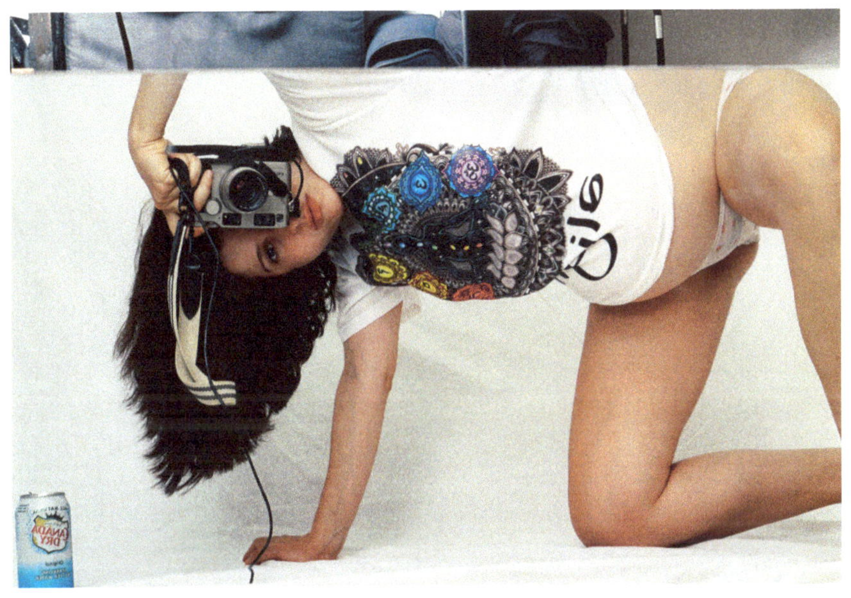

Talia Chetrit, 'Align, 2019.', from JOKE (MACK, 2022).
Courtesy of the artist and MACK.

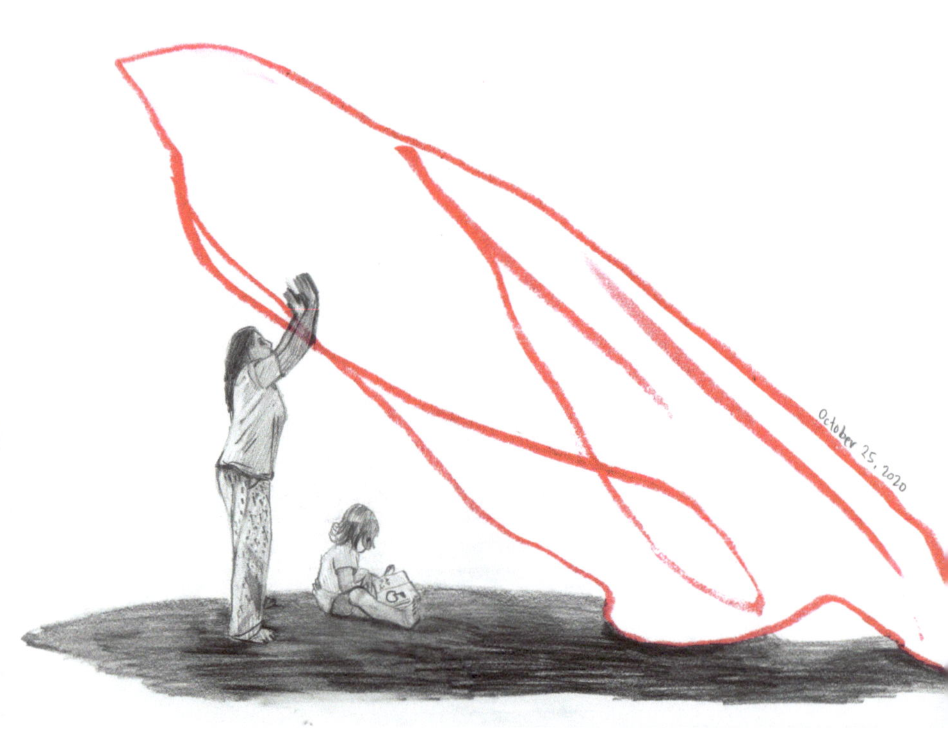
October 25, 2020

Reut **Asimini**

b. 1983 Israel

Mia & Me

2020-22

In March 2020, during the first days of the Covid-19 lockdown, interdisciplinary artist Reut Asimini found herself isolated at home with her 18-month-old daughter, Mia. It was a new reality shared by many mothers around the world: An intense proximity combined with anxiety, fear and uncertainty.

In that space, Asimini started to draw. Every evening, sitting with a pile of Mia's scribbled line drawings, she would try to intuit meanings or shapes in them that she could build upon. She says: "My maternal fascination with them, and with her, made me want to decipher her innocent lines and try to translate them."

The resulting combined drawings show aspects of their shared lives: brushing hair, vacuuming, dancing and sleeping. They're playful, sometimes silly or charming. Woven through the series, however, are images of fears and dangers, and a mother's desire for safety and joy.

reutasimini.com

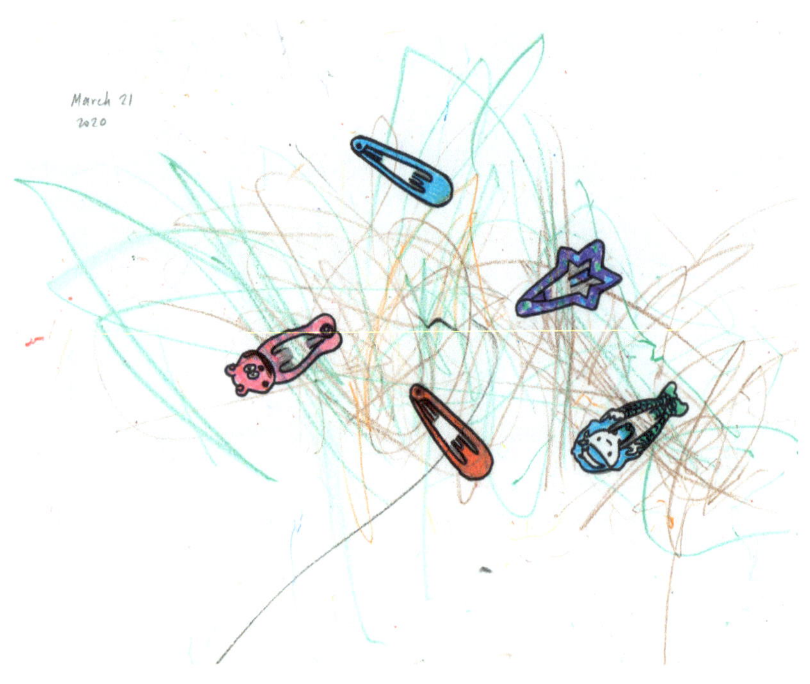
March 21
2020

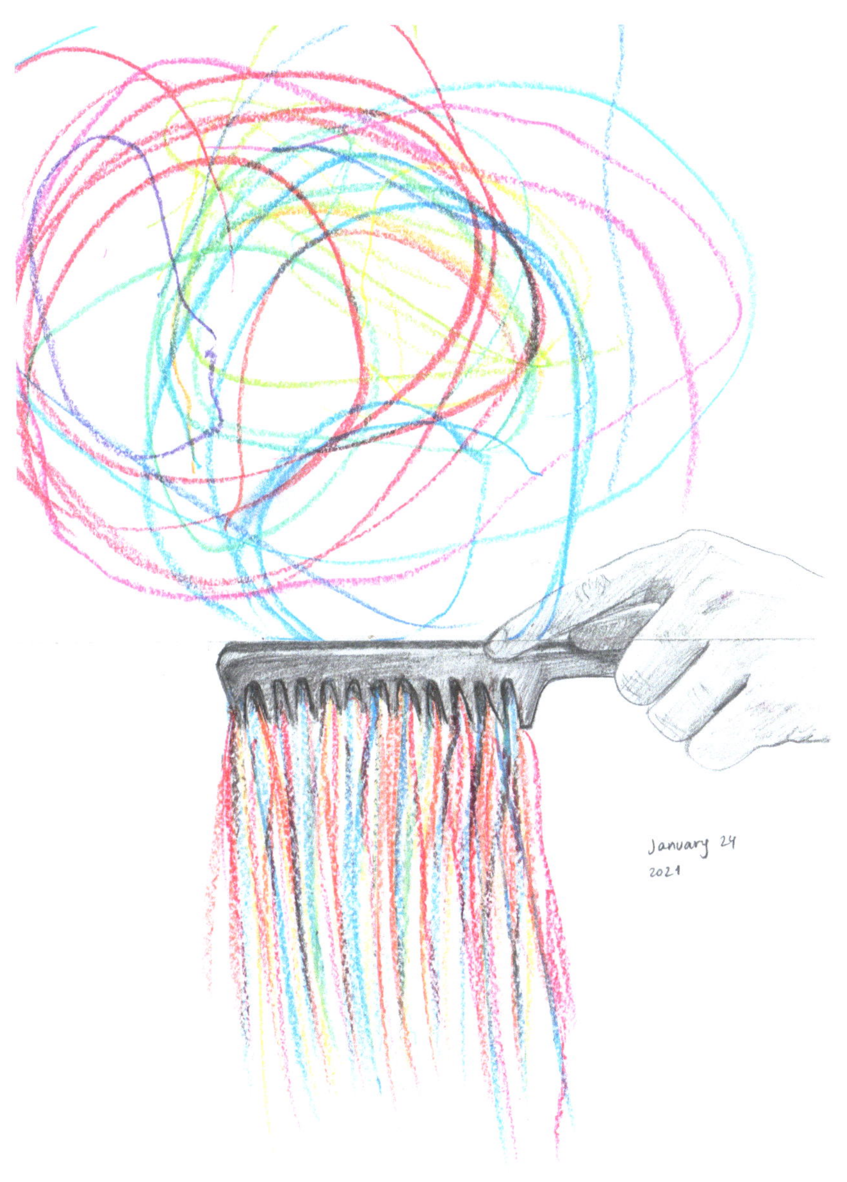

January 24
2021

Reut Asimini

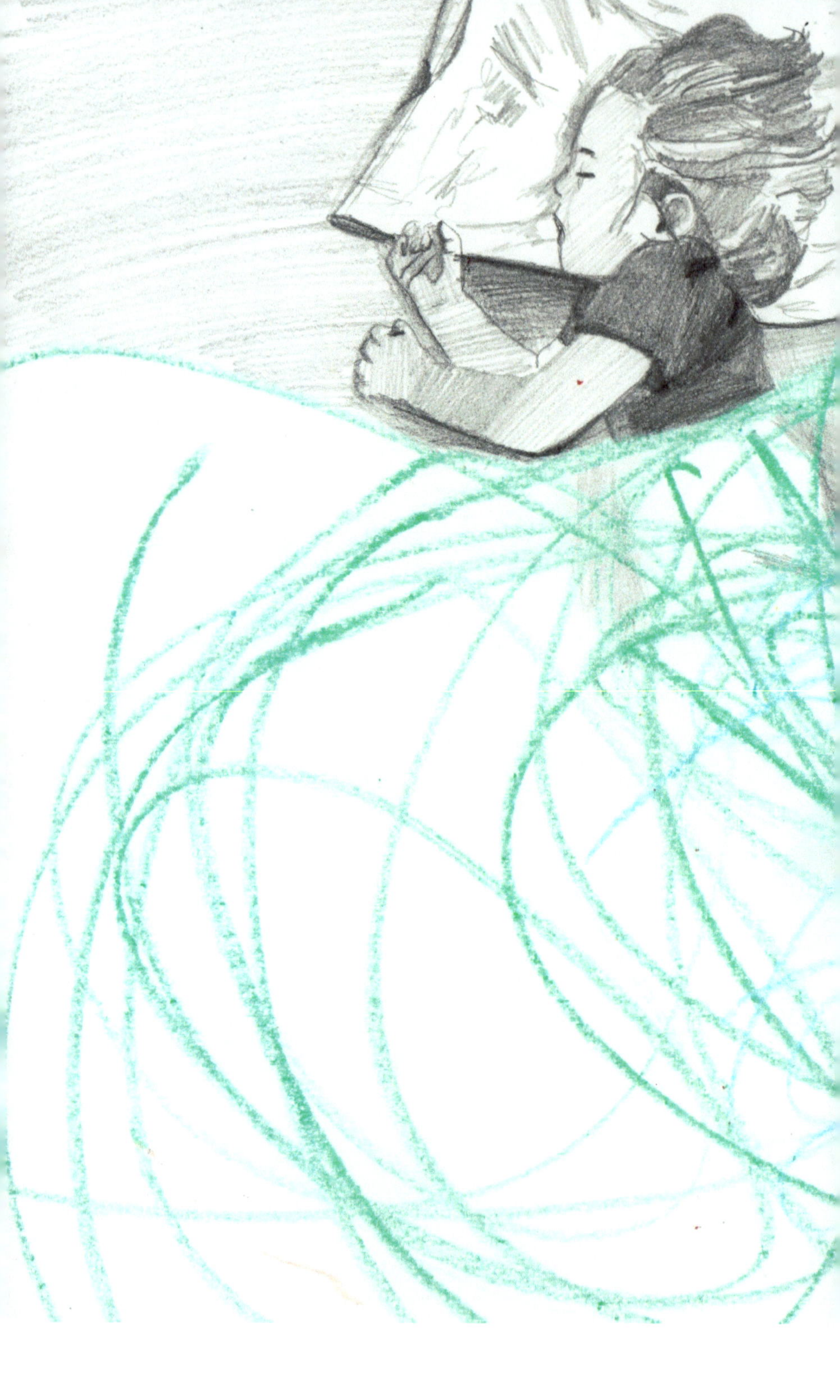

August 29
2020

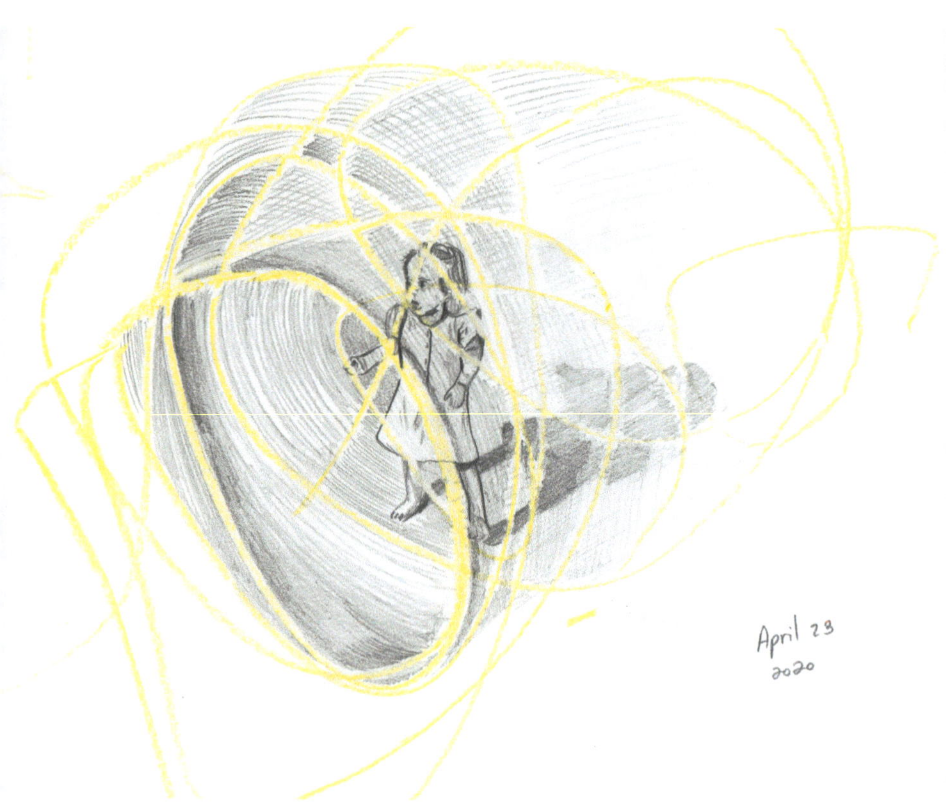

April 23
2020

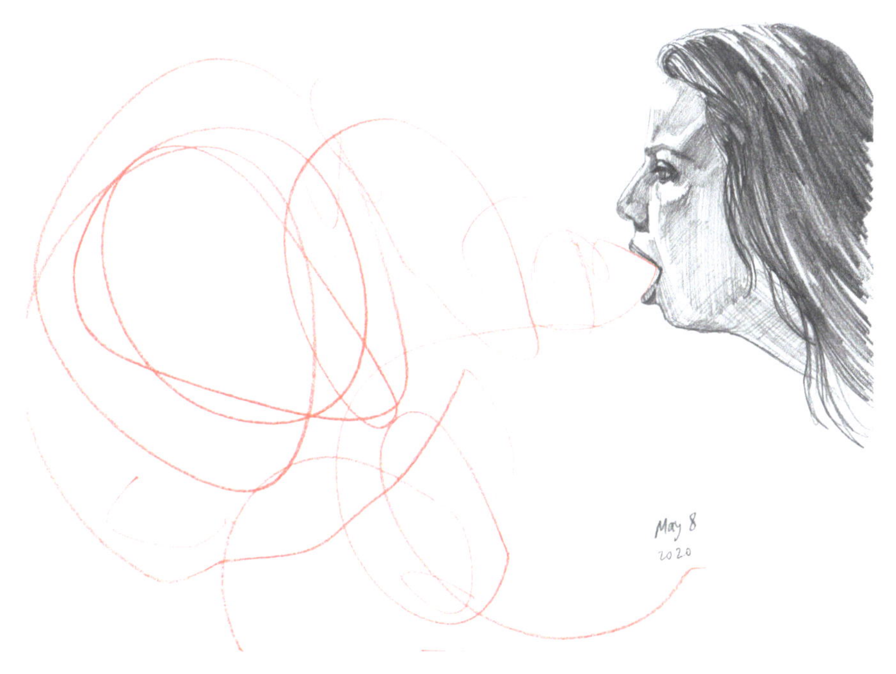

Reut Asimini

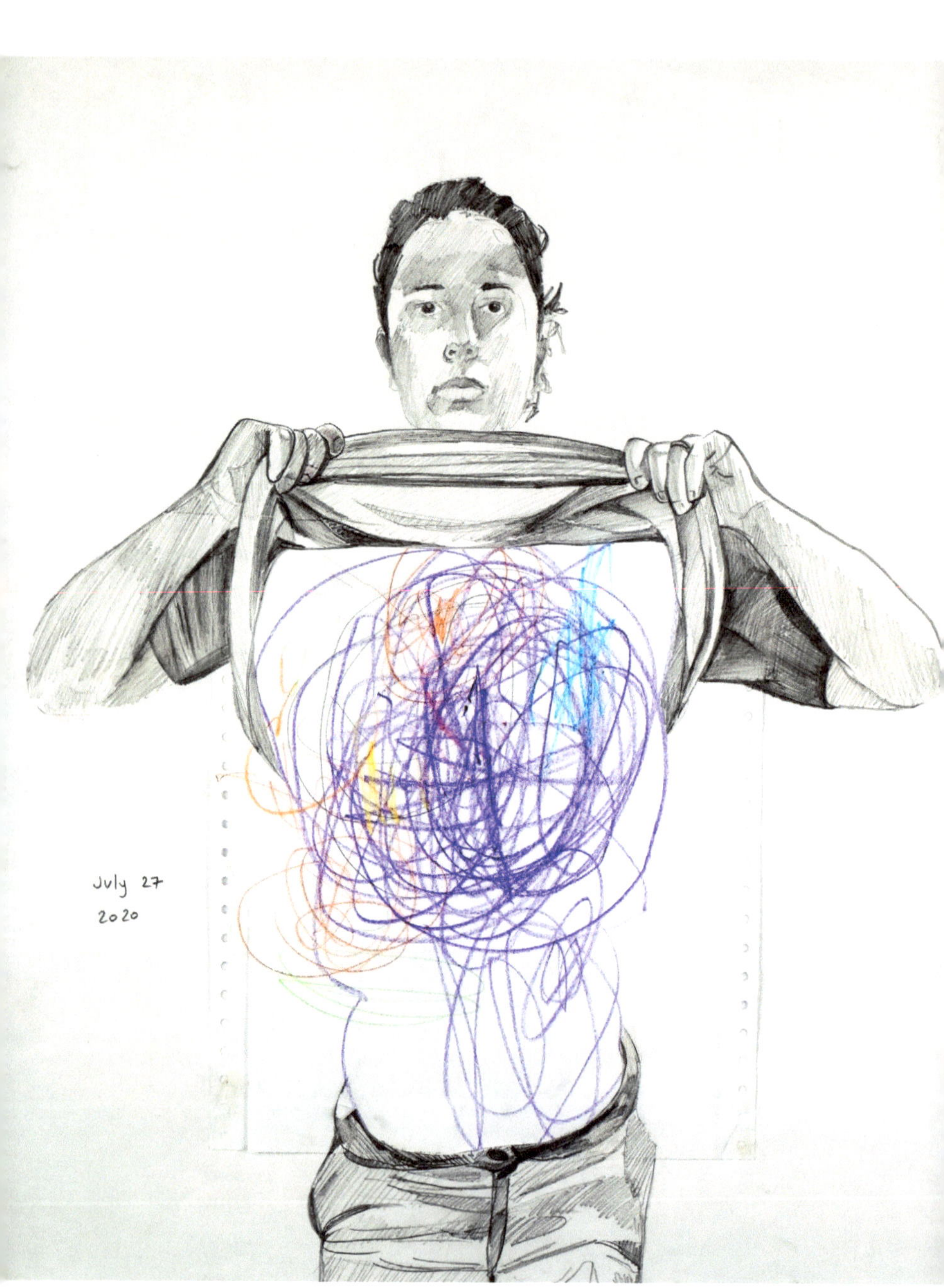
July 27
2020

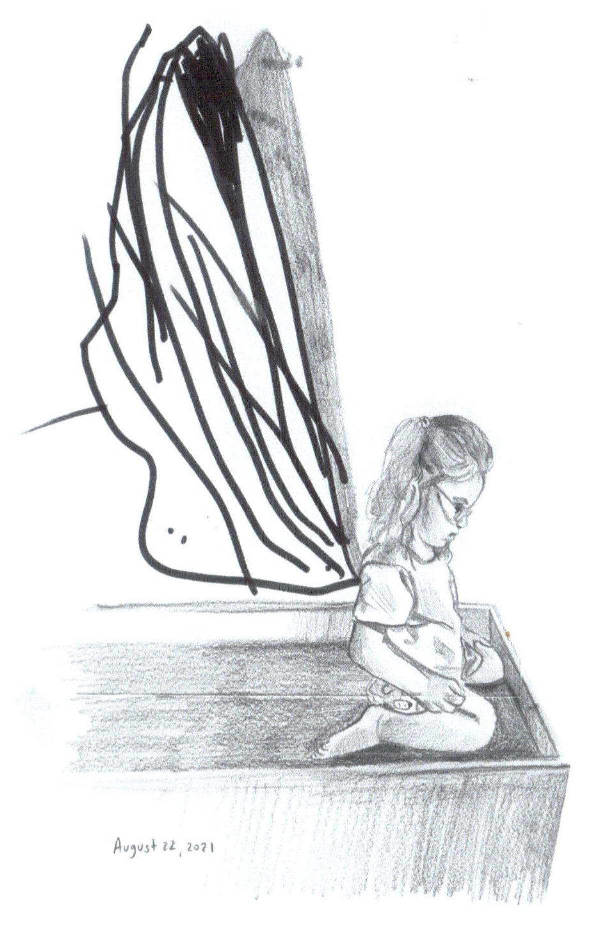

August 22, 2021

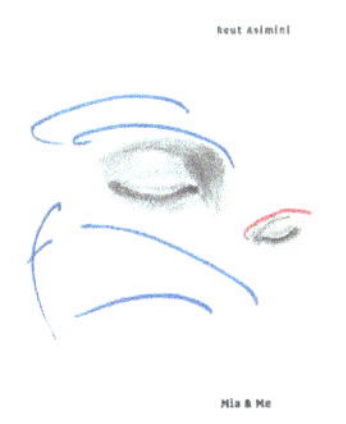

Hardback
96 pages
21 x 29 cm
Self-published, 2022
ISBN 8002110013

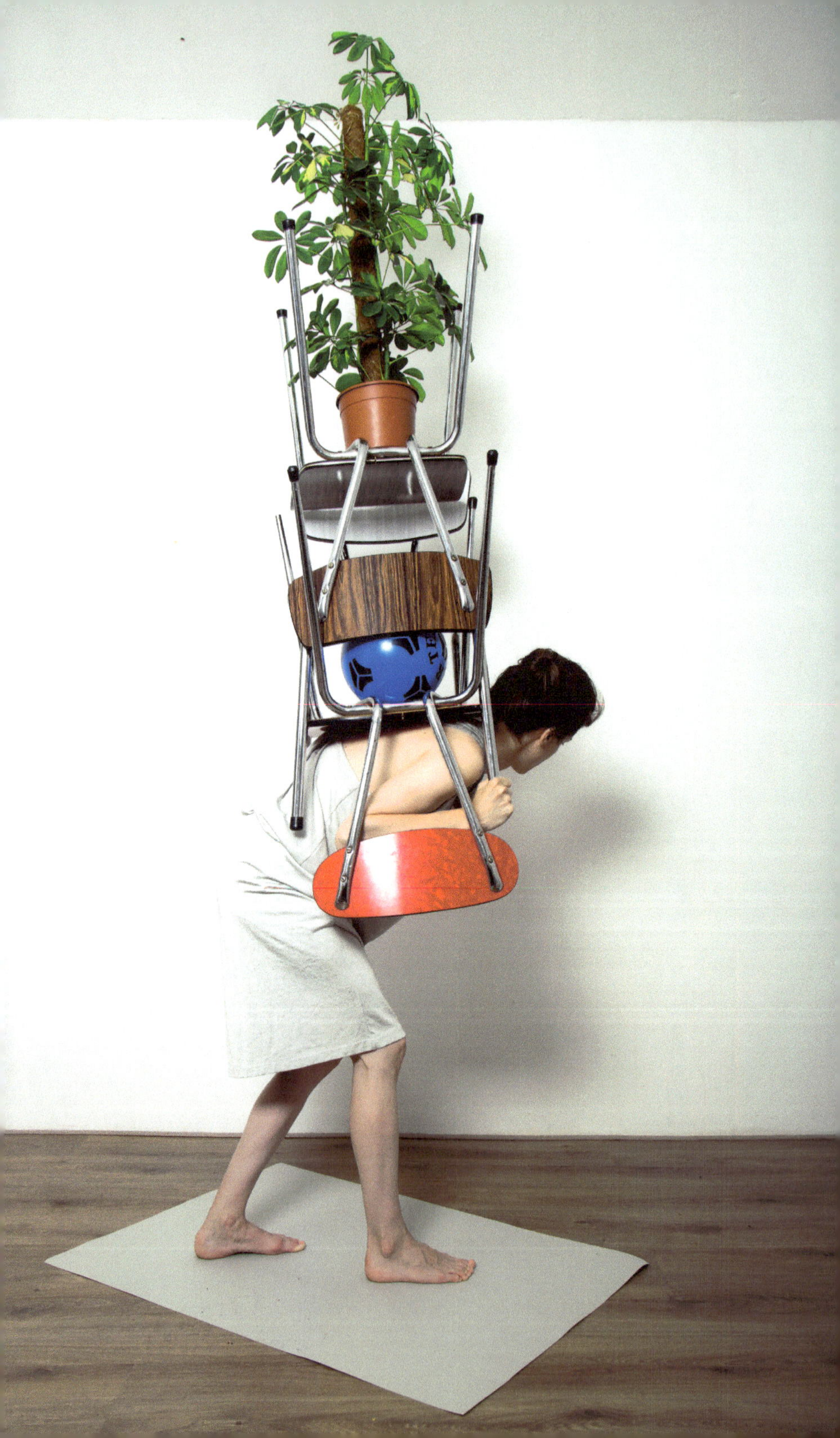

Csilla Klenyánszki

b. 1986 Hungary

Pillars of Home

Confronted with the challenges of new motherhood – caring for a fragile new life, the tension of a changing identity, not to mention a lack of time – Csilla Klenyánszki decided to transform the process into a game.

While her son napped, she had thirty minutes to transform her home into a photo studio. She constructed pillars of household objects, held in balance but unstable. The stakes were high: these impromptu assemblages could fall apart at any moment, perhaps waking a sleeping baby and putting an end to the photoshoot.

In her book *Pillars of Home*, she collects 98 of these sculptures, each filled with recognizable objects yet transformed into a strange new entity. The structures become makeshift answers to a common dilemma: "How does a mother find balance between all her priorities?"

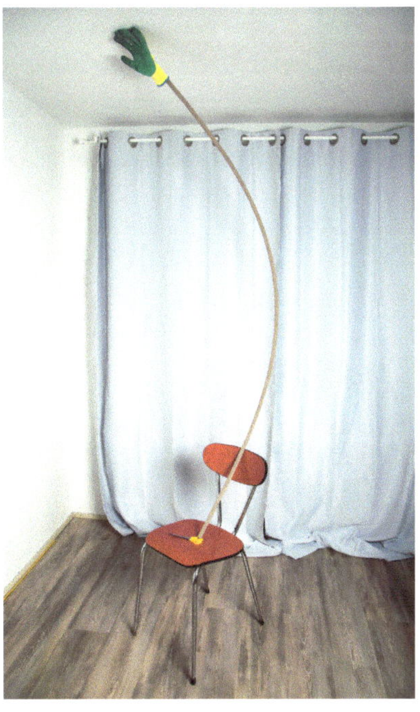

Csilla Klenyánszki

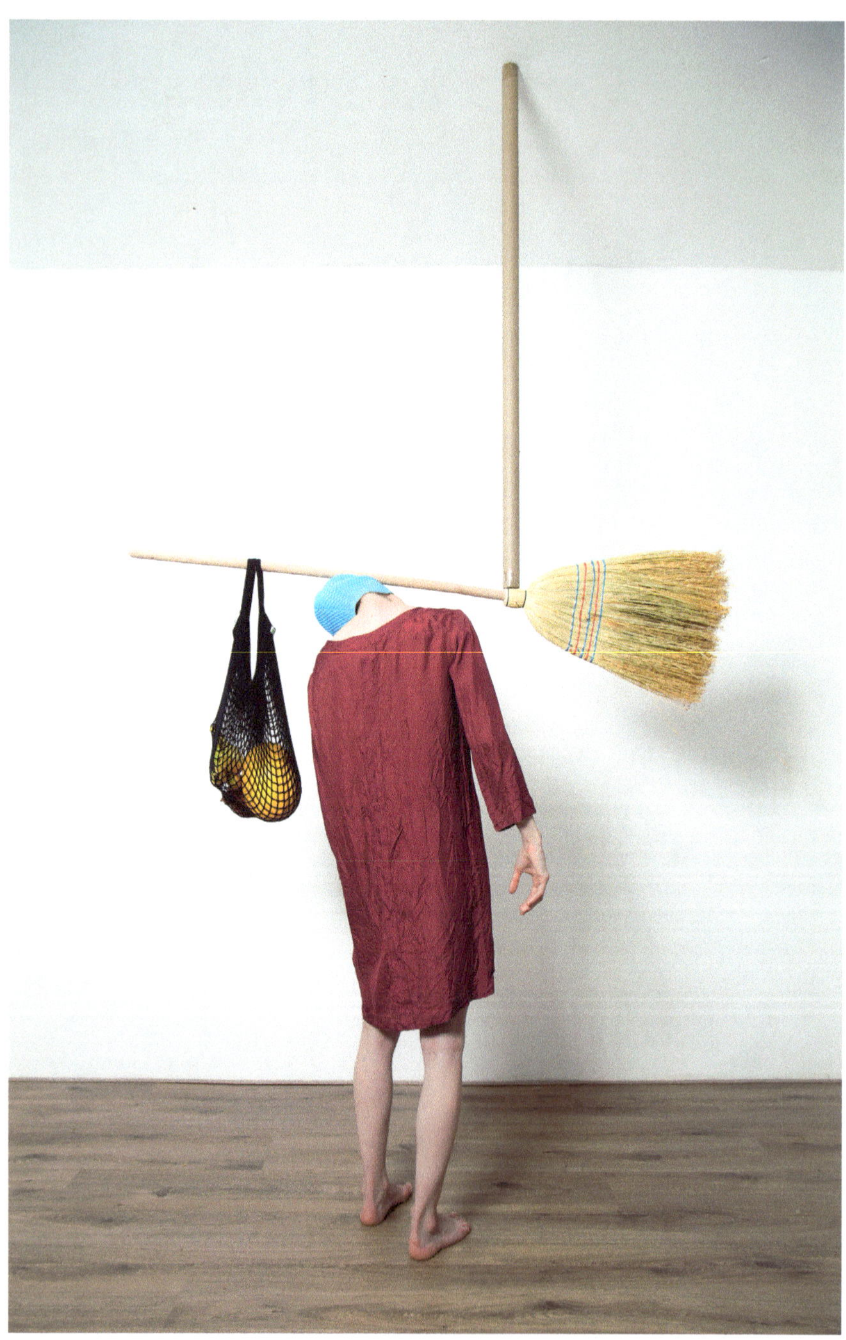

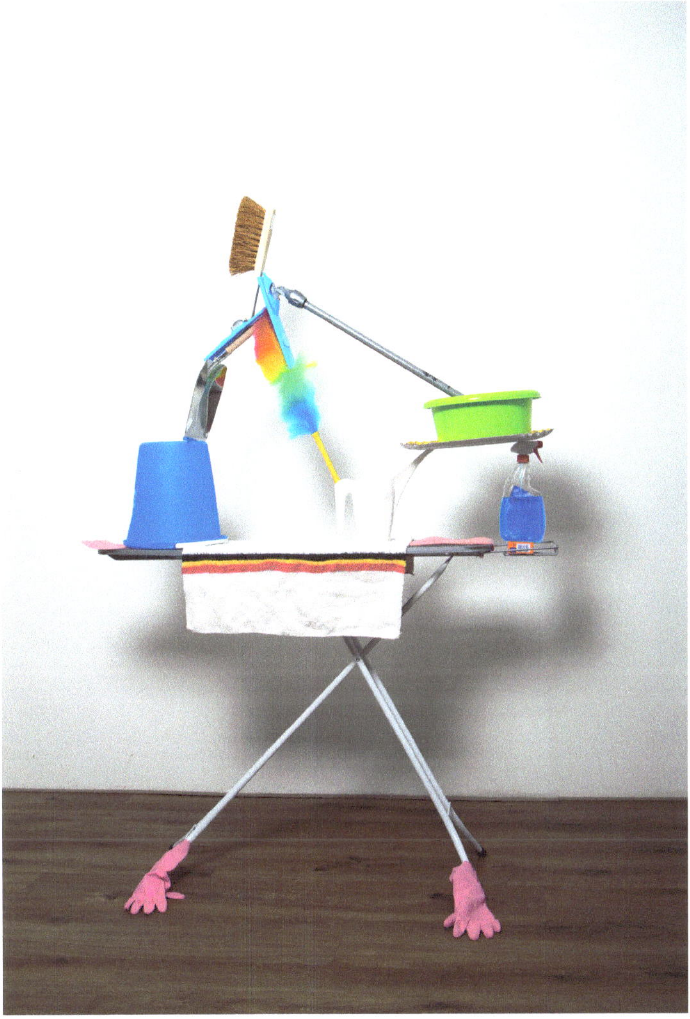

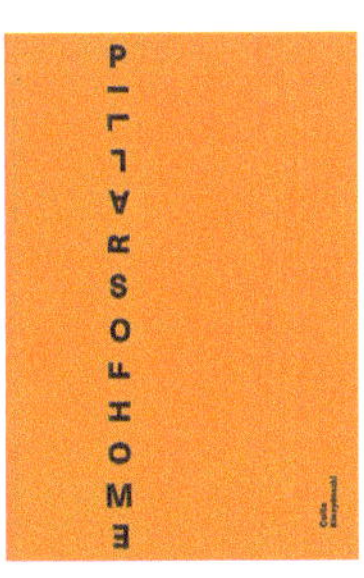

Hardback
148 pages
15 x 21 cm
Self-published, 2018
ISBN 9789082988505
€30

klenyanszki.com

In her book *The Baby on the Fire Escape:
Creativity, Motherhood, and the Mind-Baby Problem*,
Amsterdam-based author Julie Phillips looks at
the lives of an anomalous group of famous
artists of the twentieth century—women
who were both artists and mothers.

What she uncovers is a diversity of experience, with
varying degrees of happiness and success.

The book covers artists and writers including
Ursula K. Le Guin, Susan Sontag, Audre Lorde,
Doris Lessing, Angela Carter and Alice Neel. In this
interview, Julie discusses the pervasive judgment
of mothering, how interruption makes itself felt
on creativity, and the importance of being the
main character in your own story.

Julie Phillips
b. USA

Let's talk first about this metaphor of "the baby on the fire escape." What does it mean to you?
When I first did the book proposal, I realized that it needed a title. I scanned through what I'd written and there was that story about Alice Neel: Her in-laws, who were raising her child, had claimed that she'd left the baby on the fire escape to finish a painting—there wasn't any evidence for that, it was just a sign of their judgment about her as a mother. When I thought about it, it seemed to me like a really good metaphor for a space that you try to achieve with your child: far enough out of mind that you're getting your work done and close enough not to lose that bond of love and authentic connection that lets you enjoy your motherhood.

When it comes to the relationship of my writers and artists to their motherhood, I didn't want to say of them that they were 'good mothers' or 'bad mothers.' There is already so much judgment around motherhood that I didn't want to pile on more. Instead, I tried to approach it by asking: Did they enjoy it? Were they happy in their motherhood? Did it work for them? Did it put them in a better place emotionally? ...Or not.

What is it about being an artist that is so difficult to combine with motherhood?
It isn't just artistic work that's hard to combine with parenthood. I've also had letters from scientists who see themselves in the stories in my book. Of course scientific work is creative, too, in its own way; it's another form of making.

It seems to me that to write or create you need to be able to draw on yourself, the part of you that thinks its own thoughts and isn't at the service of other people's needs. Often that selfhood is equated with solitude. There's this notion of the person fully devoted to their work, whether they're alone in a room or alone wandering in the hills. I don't think you have to be *alone* to work; you can share your physical and mental space with other people. But you do need to preserve the sense of selfhood, the wellspring from which you draw, of who you are and what you are bringing to the work.

That seems to refer to what you call in the subtitle the "mind-baby problem."
Any kind of intellectual labor is seen as being canceled out by maternal labor. We associate the physical labor of motherhood with no mental engagement. In a way you do have to turn off your higher faculties to engage with a baby—who has intense use for your creativity and resourcefulness and problem-solving skills, but who is not interested in what interests you intellectually.

Your book makes the case, though, that the problem is often not just about the *baby*, but is just as much about choosing a good *partner*. You write: "A man might claim to respect a woman's talent, but seldom to the point of cooking meals or washing his own underwear."
I wrote that about male roles in the 1920s; it's much less true now. But, yes, it absolutely matters if you have people around you who are helping you, committed to helping you raise the baby, as well as good circumstances to raise your child. That doesn't have to mean a partner, per se. With Alice Neel, it was the US government, which had a subsidy program for artists during the 1930s. That steady income gave her a kind of solidity that allowed her to think about having kids again. Doris Lessing managed pretty well without partners, in part because, in that era, male partners demanded so much of the women they married. Less so of lovers, so it was a bit safer to take lovers. If you didn't know how to ask for help with parenting, if you didn't know how to *demand* that help, if your partner didn't know that it was *reasonable* to give that help, then you were better off without. But, for sure, choosing the right partner matters a lot.

The ones who were happiest in their parenting, I think, were the ones who raised kids with a loving partner and a good support network, like Audre Lorde, Ursula Le Guin, and Angela Carter. That doesn't mean you have to be monogamous, or in a traditional relationship. Other factors matter too. Alice Walker had a devoted partner, but she also had a burden of systemic racism that made her mothering much more difficult. Audre Lorde was really good at strategizing how to shelter herself from the worst effects of racism, but she flew under

"There were clearly a lot of women who chose motherhood over their art, for better or worse, and didn't make it."

the radar, while Alice Walker was more of a public figure and took all the blows that come with that when you're a black woman.

There's the elephant in the room: you're writing about the artists who did 'make it.' This selection can't include all the artists who gave up their work to be a mother, or those who didn't get acknowledged for whatever reason. What stories are left out?
Sadly, many stories. There were clearly a lot of women who chose motherhood over their art, for better or worse, and didn't make it. And a lot of women who managed to keep that flame burning while they were having children and didn't become famous, but still created things that were of value to them and the people around them. You know, you don't have to be world famous to justify your work. It can have value even if it's not in the Metropolitan Museum of Art.

Some of the women you write about, however, were very conscious of feeling like they *had* to succeed in order to justify their art, because they knew they were making sacrifices regarding their family.
Exactly. But who decides, who chooses? Why should you have to? Does something have value only because it's bringing in money? Why can't it have value because it's nourishing your soul?

I did choose to write about women who became famous because it makes it easier for people to want to read the book. But I also didn't want to write the hundredth book about Sylvia Plath or Rebecca

"I think it's normal to judge motherhood because we live with the products of it. We are ourselves the product of motherhood."

West, so I was selective, too, about who had already been written about extensively. I chose women born in the 1900s, who had thought about and written about their motherhood, or who had material that I could draw on. I would have included Toni Morrison, but I got turned down a couple of times for an interview—she was a little bit resistant, and I wasn't persistent enough.

I did feel like I was treading on intimate territory in writing about other people's motherhood. I felt a lot of trepidation entering into this subject, because it seems so private and because people are so fearful of judgment around it. I especially felt that in writing about black women's motherhood, which is a site of even more disapproval.

I felt strongly that I should portray a range of maternal experience: a diversity of economic backgrounds, a diversity of sexualities, and also racial diversity. When I started out, I had no idea what that entailed. As part of the majority culture, I didn't really think about how much I would need to know—how much I'd need to learn and read. Realizing that gave me a strong sense of responsibility to try to understand and to get everyone's story right.

We keep coming back to judgment. Why do you think that motherhood has so much judgment attached to it?
Because it's *important*. It's so fundamental to the project of human existence. I think it's normal to judge motherhood because we live with the products of it. We are ourselves the product of motherhood. If it goes wrong, it's a problem. Not just for the children but for everybody around.

So that judgment can feel intensely justified, but that doesn't mean it's right. Individual people should feel completely free to turn their backs on it, to ignore it and to go their own way. There have been excellent books written about how mothers are judged and how mothers are seen in the culture, like *Mothers* by Jacqueline Rose and *Mother of All Myths* by Aminatta Forna, but I don't think you're going to get rid of it by pointing it out. I think the motherhood police are always going to be with us. Instead you can give yourself and other people permission to step away from it, to make your own choices about what's best for you. To say, "*No*, I'm not going to have another child," or "No, I'm not going to have children at all." Or, "Yes, I'm going to put my kids in daycare." Or to say yes to more children, with or without a partner. There's so much room to do it differently. The community of mothers can be really enjoyable and supportive, and it can be mean and disapproving. It's a balance, like anything else.

You write that the idea of 'interruption' is a significant one, when it comes to motherhood and creation. Can you elaborate?
When I started reading Lisa Baraitser's book *Maternal Encounters*, about motherhood being an interrupted state of mind, I thought: *Aha! That's why I'm having such a hard time writing these essays.* I was writing a story about motherhood and a story about writing, and I just couldn't figure out how to weave these two strands together in a way that made narrative sense. It felt disjointed. The essays read like, "… And then this happened, and then this happened, and then this happened." But that struck me as feeling very much like motherhood itself, a list of events and anecdotes. Baraitser's book made me think about motherhood not as something that women *did*, but as a *state* of interrupted consciousness.

It's a little bit upsetting to us, as the audience, to think about writers and artists having an interrupted consciousness or an interrupted day. I think when we're looking at a work of art, or reading a book, and feeling completely involved or immersed, we want to think of the creator as being likewise completely involved. That's part of the fantasy of the 'art monster' who's completely devoted to the work—it's the artist completely devoted to *you*. You don't want to have to think about them turning away in the middle of it to get dinner for their kid. You don't want to have to share.

Indeed, art is appreciated for its otherworldliness and abstraction, while motherhood and domestic duties are very grounded even when filled with awe. You write in the book: "The sublime is twinned with the banal in mothering." It puts mothering artists at a disadvantage—at least in terms of how we perceive them.
Yeah, how can art be transcendent when the conditions of making it are so quotidian? It's ironic to think that the devotion we're seeking from an artist is really a kind of maternal devotion to the work.

Seeing interruption as potentially *productive*, and as a natural condition of the writing, was important to me because I did feel frustrated by second-wave feminism, which talked about motherhood in terms of trying to get the conditions right—you know, when there are crèches and partners sharing the work, then writing and mothering will take place in harmony. It just doesn't happen that way. You're still doing that work of mothering and it's still impinging on and altering your consciousness.

Part of what put me on the path to finishing the book was rereading something that Ursula Le Guin said, which was that she didn't see how a mother could be a hero. She felt like those two were mutually exclusive. I just felt an intense emotional resistance to that statement—it made me mad. I realized the only way to make these essays work was to see these women as heroes of their own motherhood. As the central character and as the authors of their own lives.

Your own children are now grown, but did you learn anything through the artists you wrote about that changed how you approached your work?
I had trouble with the empty nest, and I'm still finding it a bit difficult to regain my rhythm. Even when my children got just a little bit older, maybe seven and four, and were not as physically dependent on me, I missed that a lot. I found that really painful. That coincided with me finishing my first book and feeling a little lost with not having a new project. I always thought: *If you're a really great writer, you're not going to have a problem with the empty nest, because you have your writing to go back to.* It turns out that it's upending for everyone. All the artists I wrote about had trouble with it.

"Part of the selfhood that is necessary for a writer is being able to make choices about how physically present you want to be in your motherhood and not have those choices be determined for you by other people."

You write in the book, "Reproductive rights—including access to abortion, contraception, fertility treatment, and health care—are a necessary part of creative mothering." You dedicate a lot of page space to this, which is worth mentioning because multiple artists in your book had abortions early on in their lives but then went on to have a family later, illustrating that it wasn't a matter of 'if' so much as 'when'.

To have some control over the timing and the circumstances was so valuable for them. It makes such a difference if you have enough money to raise a child, if you have healthcare for your child and for yourself, if you feel supported in the circumstances of having children, and not worked against at every turn by people who think *they* should determine the timing of your children and how hard you should work before you deserve healthcare and daycare.

As a mother, you do lose a massive amount of bodily autonomy. I could've written even more about bodies and motherhood except that I didn't want to essentialize too much. I didn't want to leave out all the people who didn't become mothers through pregnancy, who didn't nurse, who didn't have those bodily experiences that we think of as 'essential' to motherhood, because really nothing is essential to motherhood. Mother is as mother does, as Angela Carter said.

Part of the selfhood that is necessary for a writer is being able to make choices about how physically present you want to be in your motherhood, and not have those choices be determined for you by other people. Methods like 'attachment parenting' deliver a loss of bodily autonomy – and you can of course *choose* that, if you want,

"Usually it's
lots of little choices
and it's seldom one big choice."

but that's very different than being made to feel guilty if you choose *not* to do that, or being made to feel that you're doing harm to your baby if you're not present all the time. Likewise, to have to hand your baby over to daycare at six weeks so that you can go back to work, if that's not what you want, is also a terrible loss of autonomy.

But the thing about the loss of bodily autonomy is that it does pass. You do get yourself back physically as your kids get older.

What do you wish that more people would know or understand before becoming artist-mothers?
I wish the idea was more widely accepted for mothers to see themselves as being at the center of their own story – as being on a hero's journey. That story is so absent from the way people talk about motherhood, that you don't even realize that it's not there. I didn't see it until I started thinking biographically about motherhood. When other people are making demands on you, it can be hard to see yourself as the main character of your own story, or at least that's true for me. I drift along in my own life if I don't make a major effort to think: *I am the actor. I'm doing this.*

To think about motherhood as a story is to put yourself at the center, to observe what it demands of you and the ways in which you take or yield control, and to be aware of how it changes you. So, that's what I wish people would know: that becoming a mother isn't something that happens, it's something you do. It's your adventure.

Your book starts with the story of Alice Neel, which is quite a tragic story because she's confronted with a large choice of whether or not to abandon her child to be an artist. Hopefully this is somewhat rare – that a person would be forced to choose one or the other outright – and most are faced instead with

much smaller, daily choices. Whether to work on the oil painting or enjoy playtime, let's say. How are we to choose?

Yes, usually it's lots of little choices and it's seldom one big choice. Alice Neel's story was hard to write because, at first, I thought it was the story of that choice, but really, hers is the story of *living with* that choice. It's what she made of that choice, and how she tried to recoup or undo that choice by having two more children. Not everybody has the psychological gifts to solve all their parenting problems. Not everybody is able to do the needed psychic repair work, or even to see clearly the damage done as something that has happened to your child and not only to yourself.

Originally, I started this book wanting to write about women who had left their children in order to write. I had a clear idea of the contrast between mothering and writing, because I felt like writing is always leaving your child in a certain sense. So, I thought by examining those writers' stories, I could get at the essence of that feeling of guilt and freedom that you have when you take time to yourself. But I don't think that's true. I don't think it's in those big stories of abandonment, I think it's in the stories where you have to do it daily.

How have you made it work in your life?

I was lucky enough to get to live in the Netherlands for the last 28 years, where I had subsidized daycare and affordable rent. I was lucky enough to have a partner who really believed in what I was doing. All those things gave me what I needed: the implicit assumption that I, as a writer, was still entitled to my time, even if it wasn't generating money at that moment.

julie-phillips.com

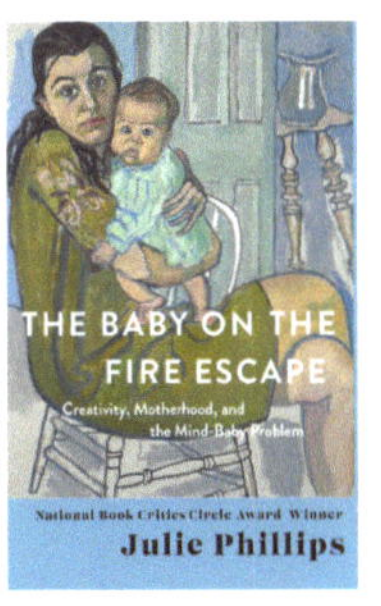

Hardback
320 pages
15.5 x 23.5 cm
W. W. Norton, 2022
ISBN 9780393088595
$28

wwnorton.com

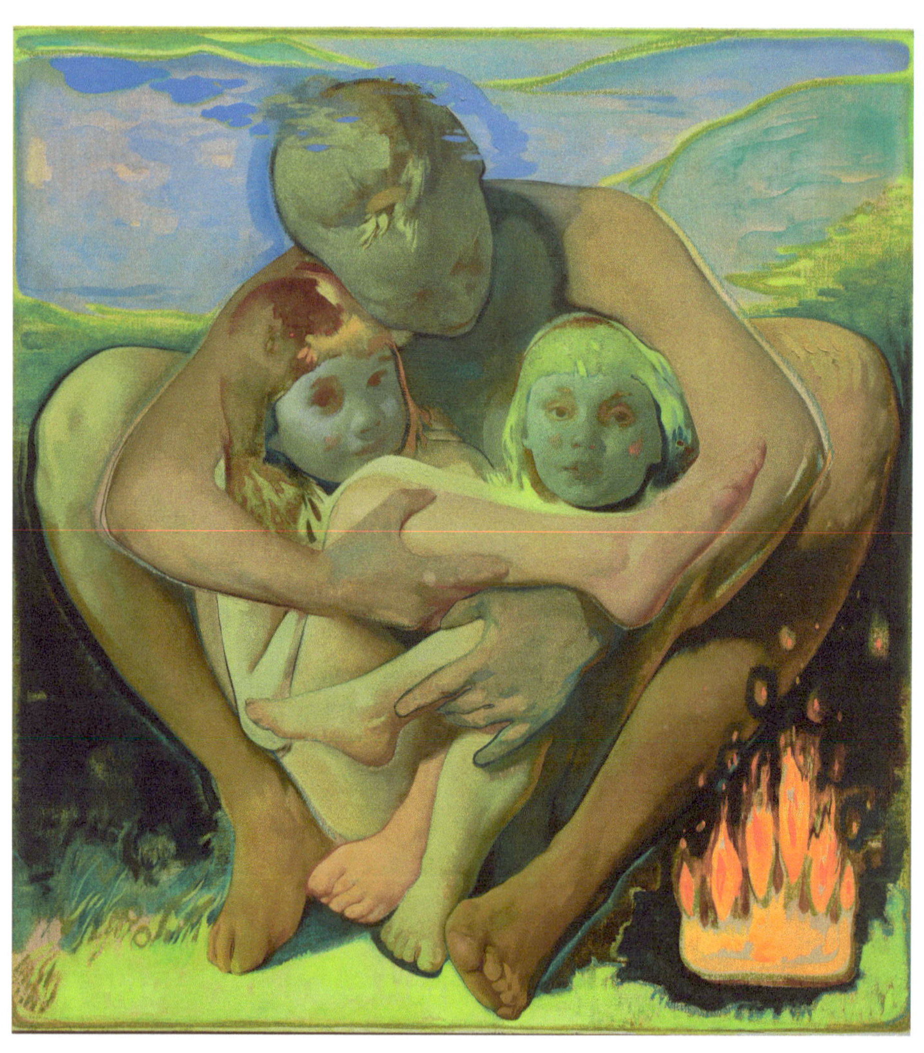

TAKE THIS FIRE (2022)
40 x 42 inches, oil and pigment sticks on linen.
Private Collection NYC.

Colleen **Barry**
b. 1981 USA

Works on Motherhood
2021-22

Colleen Barry brings the studied skill of European Masters into the modern day with her bold, playful style. In this selection of paintings, we see the timeless themes of motherhood, protection, and courage. Bodies touch, flesh against flesh. The mother envelopes her offspring, part cuddle and part huddle, hands and feet interlocked. Since becoming a mother, she says, her work transitioned away from portraits and more towards the figure. She writes: "I found the body could express ideas surrounding motherhood in a stronger, more powerful way."

Barry draws inspiration from ancient symbolism and myths as well as current events. She began painting *Lupa*, one of two paintings that reference the mythological she-wolf, on the day of the school shooting in Uvalde, Texas in 2022. She says: "These works took on a new meaning and significance to me about what it means to be a protector of the innocent."

Animalistic and humanist, classical and daring, Barry's paintings are equal parts sensitive and primal.

colleenbarryart.com

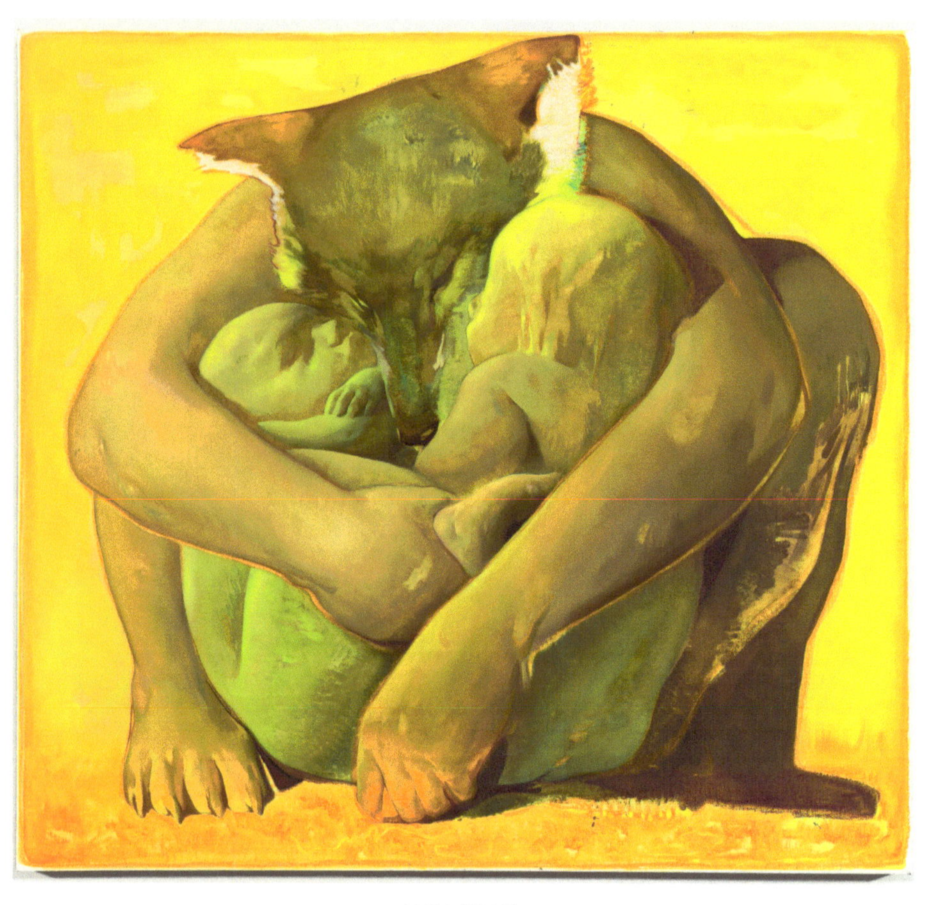

LUPA (2022)
51 x 46 inches, oil and pigment sticks on linen.
Private Collection NYC.

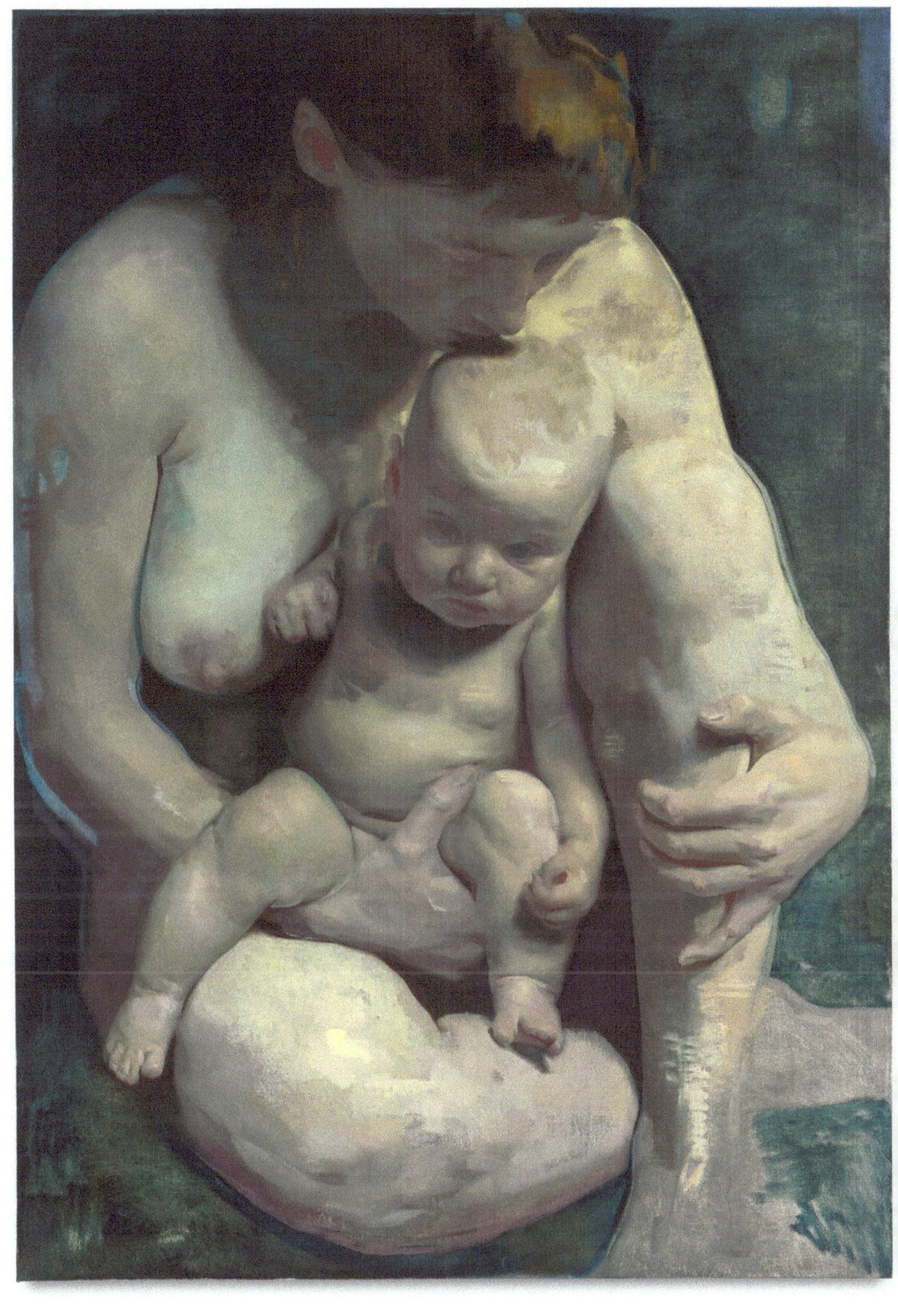

HAVEN (2021)
36 x 50 inches, oil on linen.
Private Collection CA.

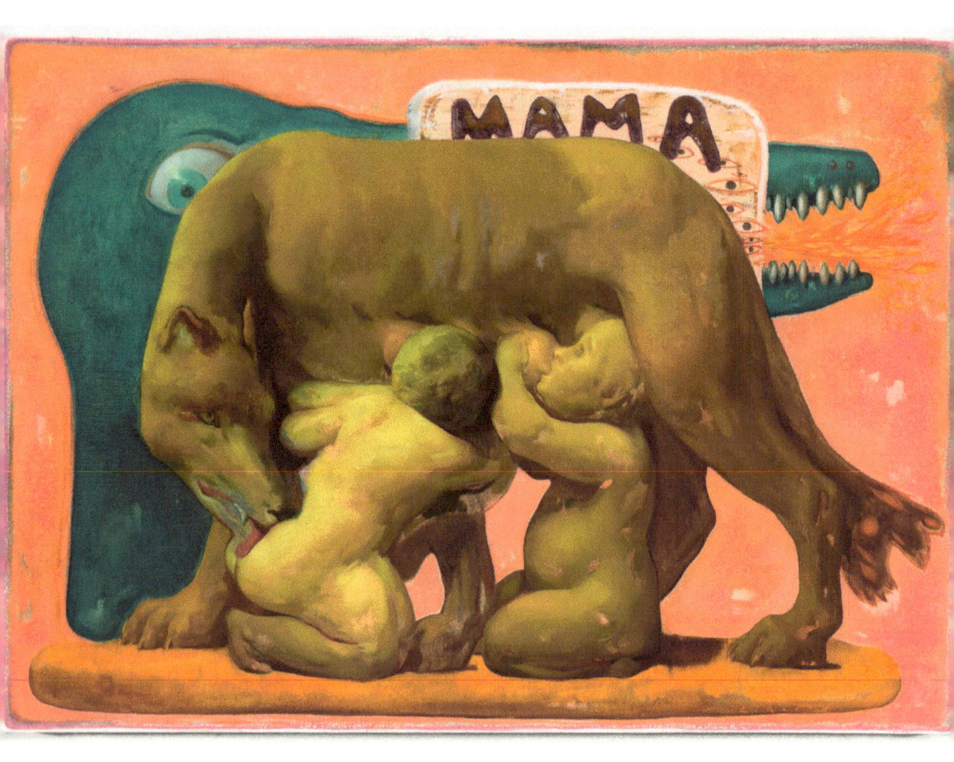

MAMA (2022)
40 x 28 inches, oil and pigment sticks on linen.
Private Collection NYC.

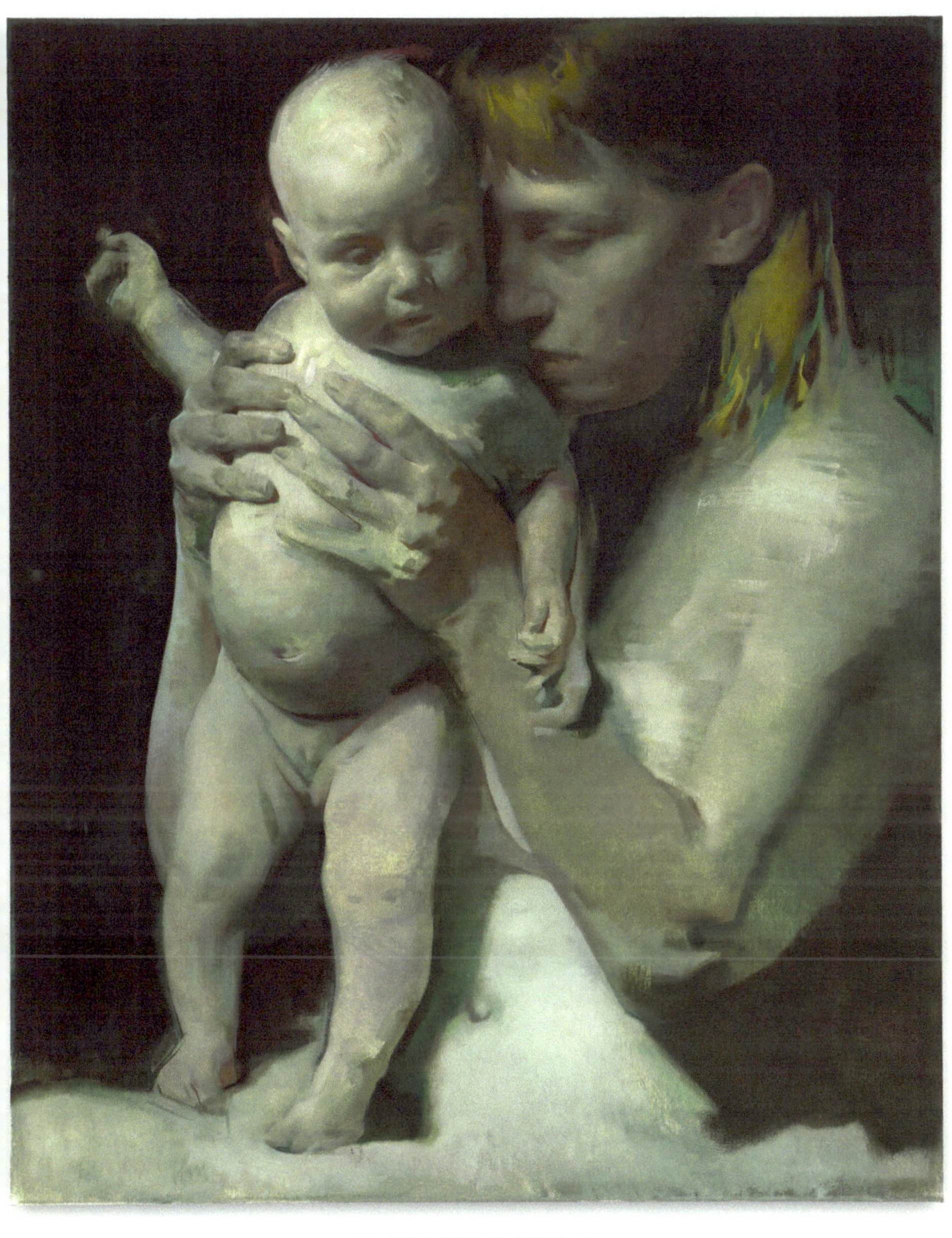

LOVE AND YOUTH (2020)
46 x 56 inches, oil on linen.
Private Collection CA.

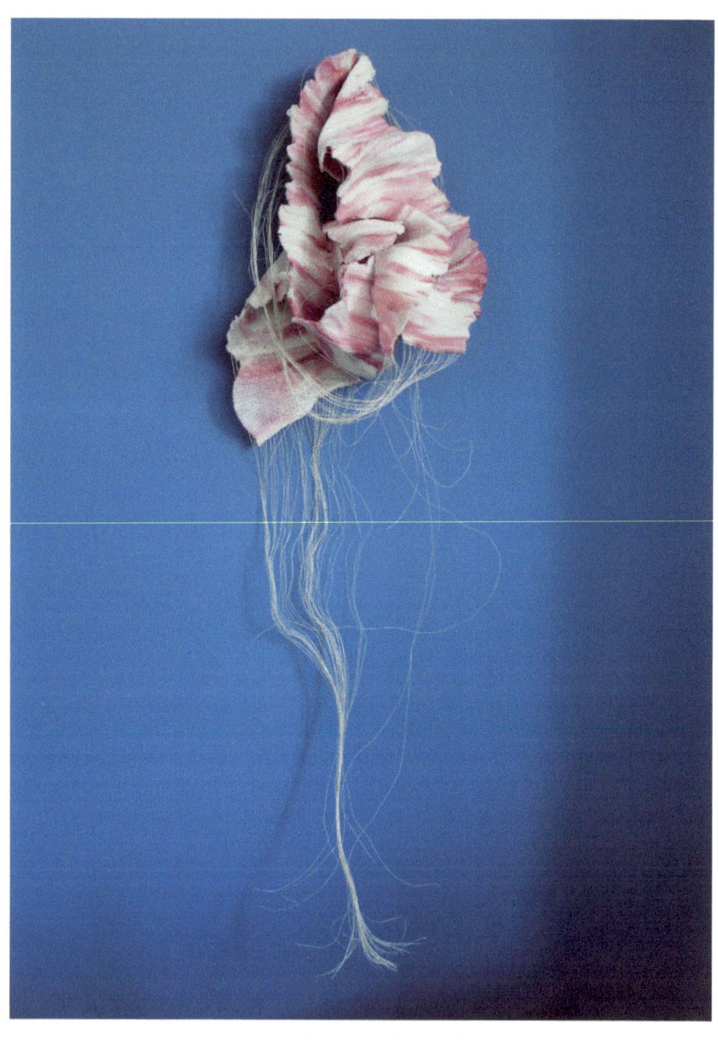

Fluid Garland (2020)
30 wet-wipes pleated with wire, naturally dyed and embroidered

Kath **Lovett**

b. 1979 UK

Wet Wipe Activism

2020-21

Textile artist Kath Lovett works with everyday wet wipes, ubiquitous in childrearing and imbued with the connotations of cleaning and caregiving, as a medium to explore feminist ideas around domestic labor.

Lovett processes the wipes through a method she invented, using a princess-pleater, traditionally used for smocking, to add bulk to the fabric using threads of cotton or wire. She accents the wet wipes with household dyes: beetroot peelings from borscht soup, which her grandmother made, and raspberry tea, which her children like to drink.

The resulting figures appear organic—ironically so, since most wet wipes are made of polyester that takes hundreds of years to biodegrade, despite being single-use items. Lovett also hopes that her usage of the material raises awareness about the harmful environmental impact of wipes.

kathlovett.com

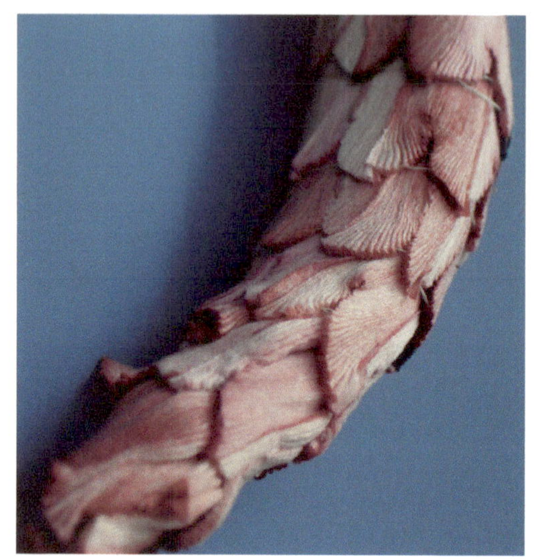

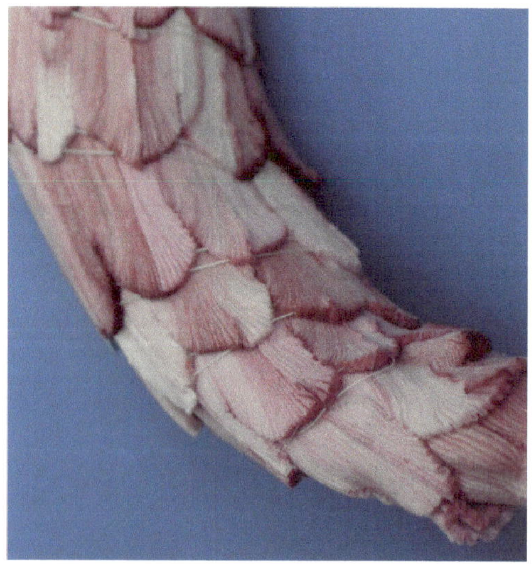

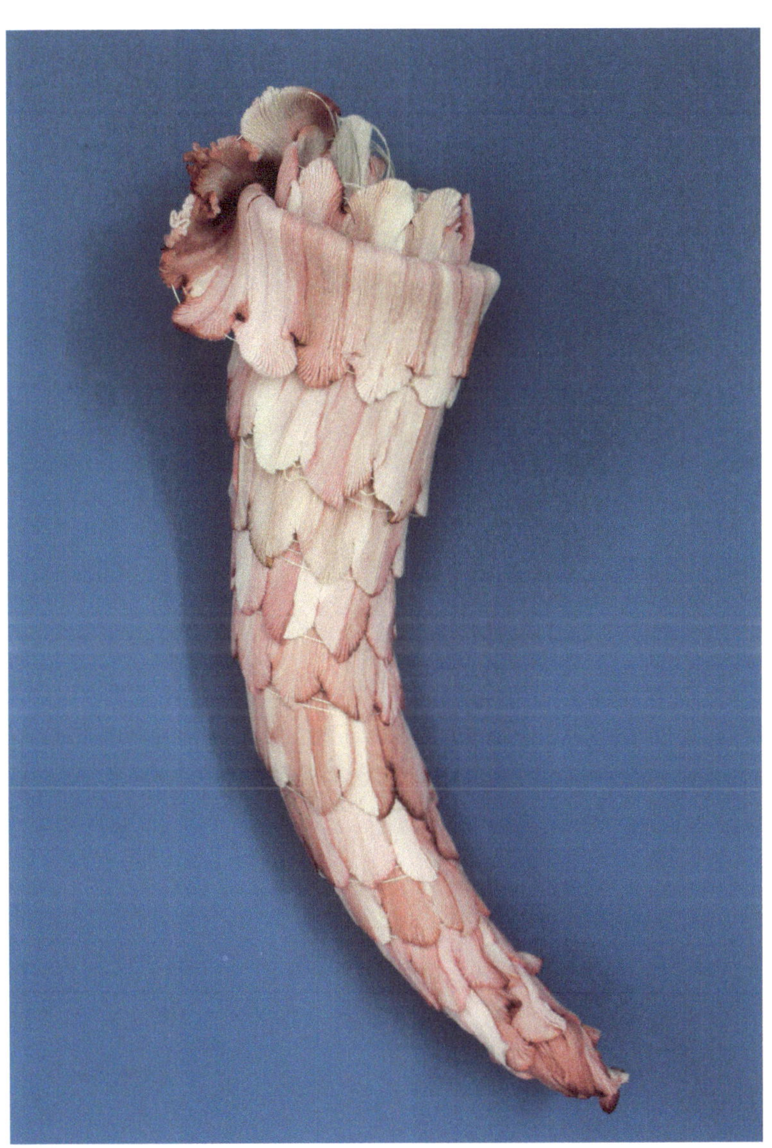

Compressed Labour (2020)
151 baby-wipes, natural dyes, thread.

Each wipe represents a single message sent from my son's school
Whatsapp group over a half term: 148 messages from the female carers
and 3 from the male carers. The wipes are pleated as tightly as possible,
the emotional labor of each individual message rendered nearly invisible.

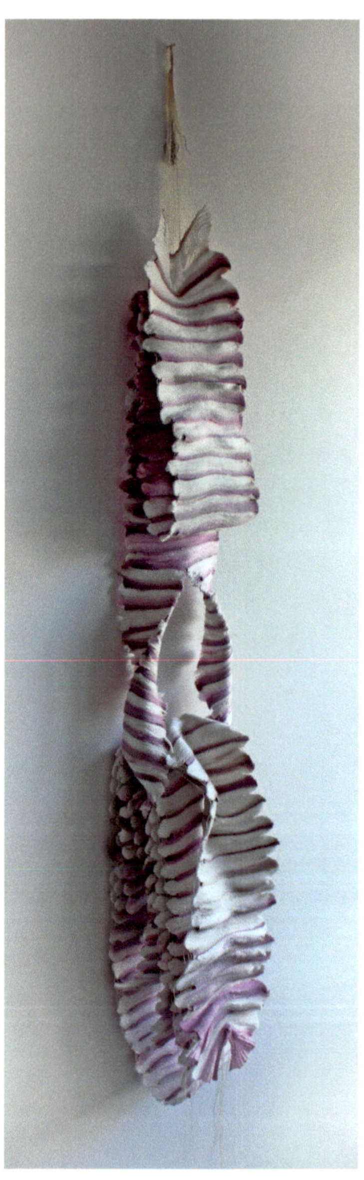

132 Months (2020)
132 baby-wipes, dip dyed with beetroot and raspberry tea, hand-pleated with the smocking needles remaining in the piece.

Each baby wipe signifies a month of mothering, the weight of the piece pulling at the pin that holds it together, like the burden of expectations. The lengthy process to make the piece is integral to its meaning: it is about hidden labor, like the endless folding and sorting of piles of clothes which makes up much of my day.

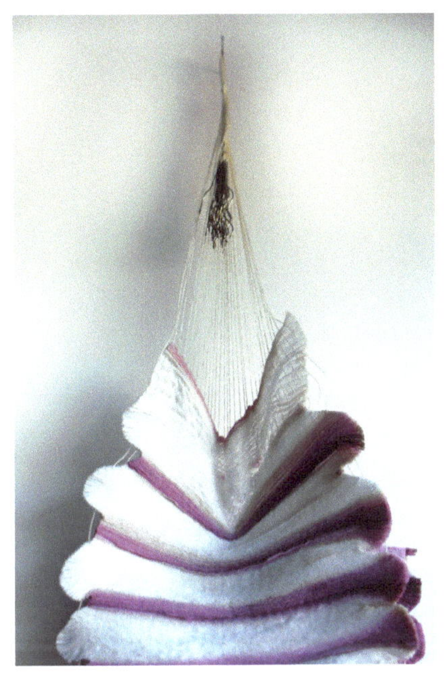

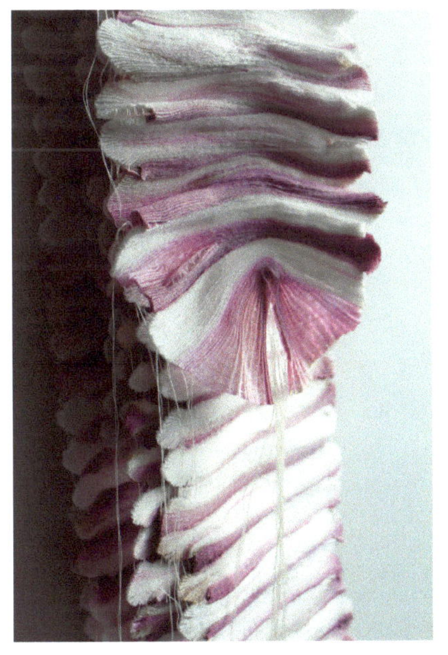

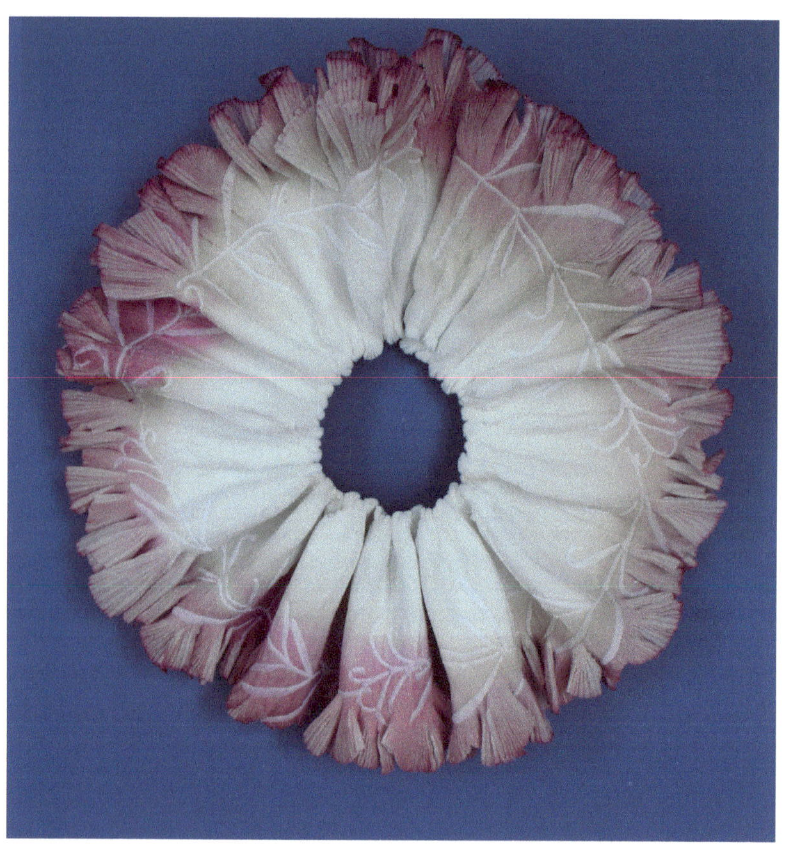

Totem for Sleep (2021)
Baby-wipes, natural dyes, thread.

This wreath is a response to my daughter's poor sleep over the last year, coinciding with the first lockdown and only now getting back to some normality. It's made from 45 pleated wipes, for the 45 weeks of no sleep, and embroidered with drawings of the rosemary that I placed under her pillow to help her sleep.

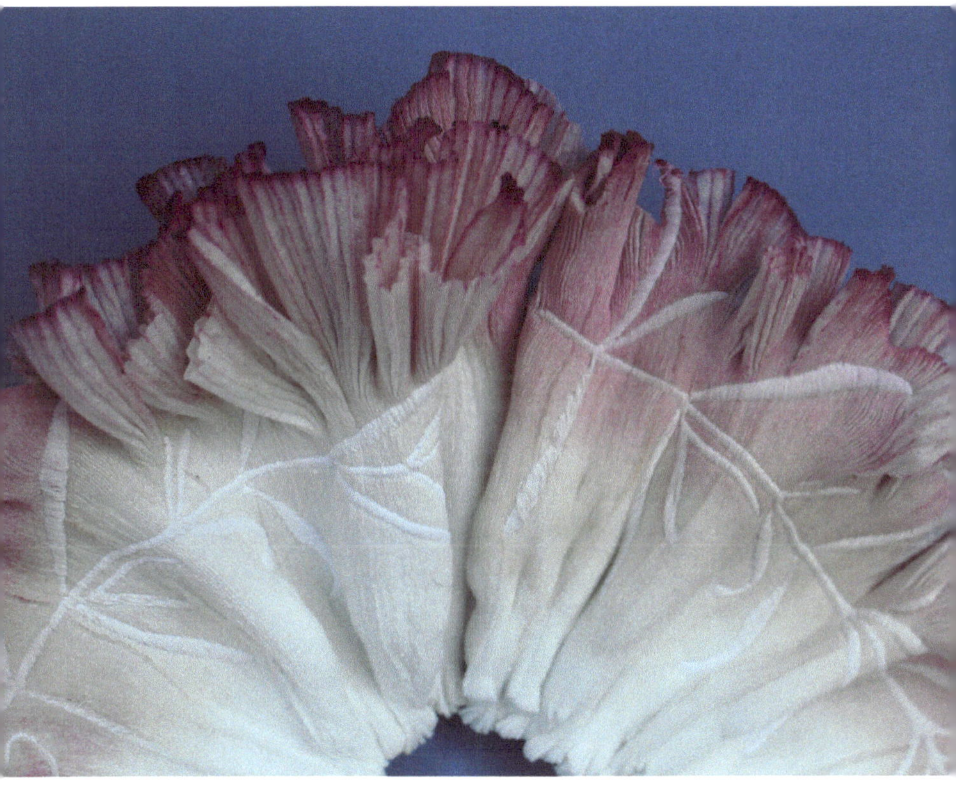

Kath Lovett

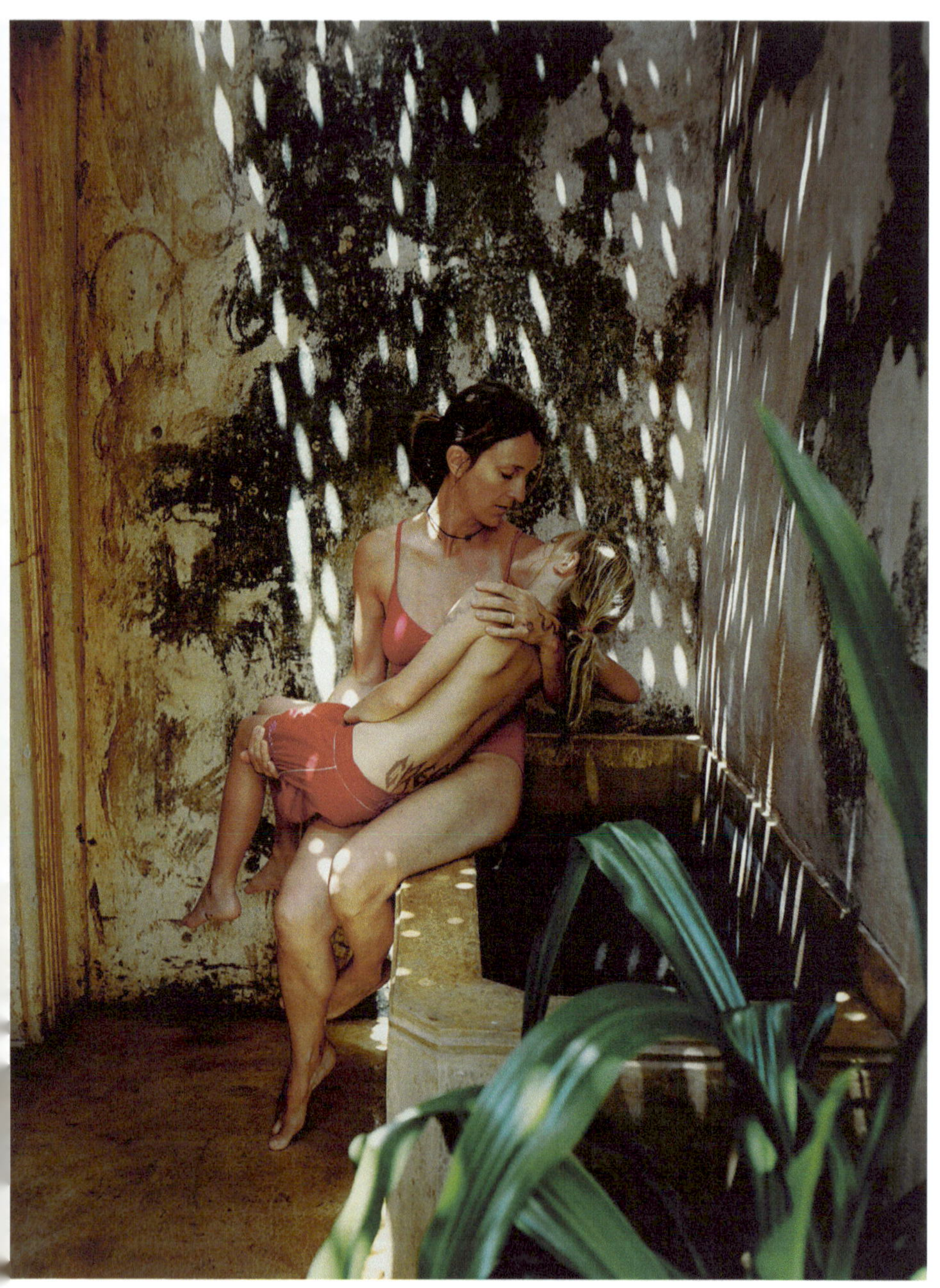

pietà in red swimsuits

Emma Hardy

Permissions

The spaces where a family spends time are transformed by something ineffable: locations interweave with memory, a house becomes a home. Even an anonymous hotel room becomes familiar.

Emma Hardy tells the touching story of her family through its long relationship with a home in *Permissions*, a book of photographs spanning twenty years. The project finds its roots in the family selling the house and their shared history of memories there coming to a close. Though the images are divorced from any timeline – they're neither sequential nor marked by date – we see the progression of three generations as the years flit back and forth. And, in an homage to the loss of the house, Hardy records still lifes of flowers at various stages of blossoming and wilting during that final spring spent in the garden.

Confronted with the end of an era, minor details of daily life take on new meaning. Sunshine is infused with the fleeting beat of time, and memories feel lost and found again.

emmahardy.com

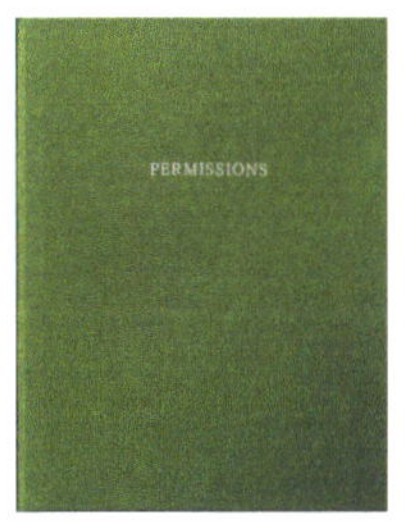

Hardback
160 pages
24.5 x 30.6 cm
GOST Books, Nov. 2022
ISBN 9781910401781
€45 / £40 / $50

gostbooks.com

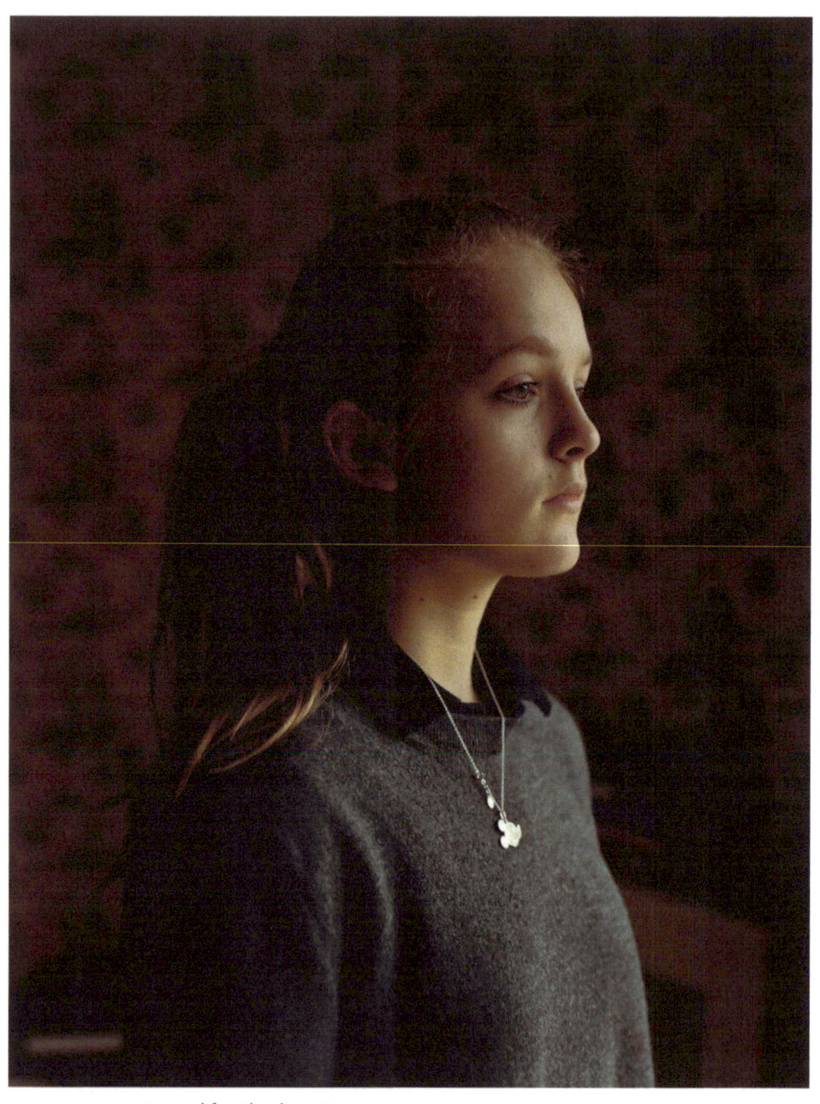

unpierced for the last time

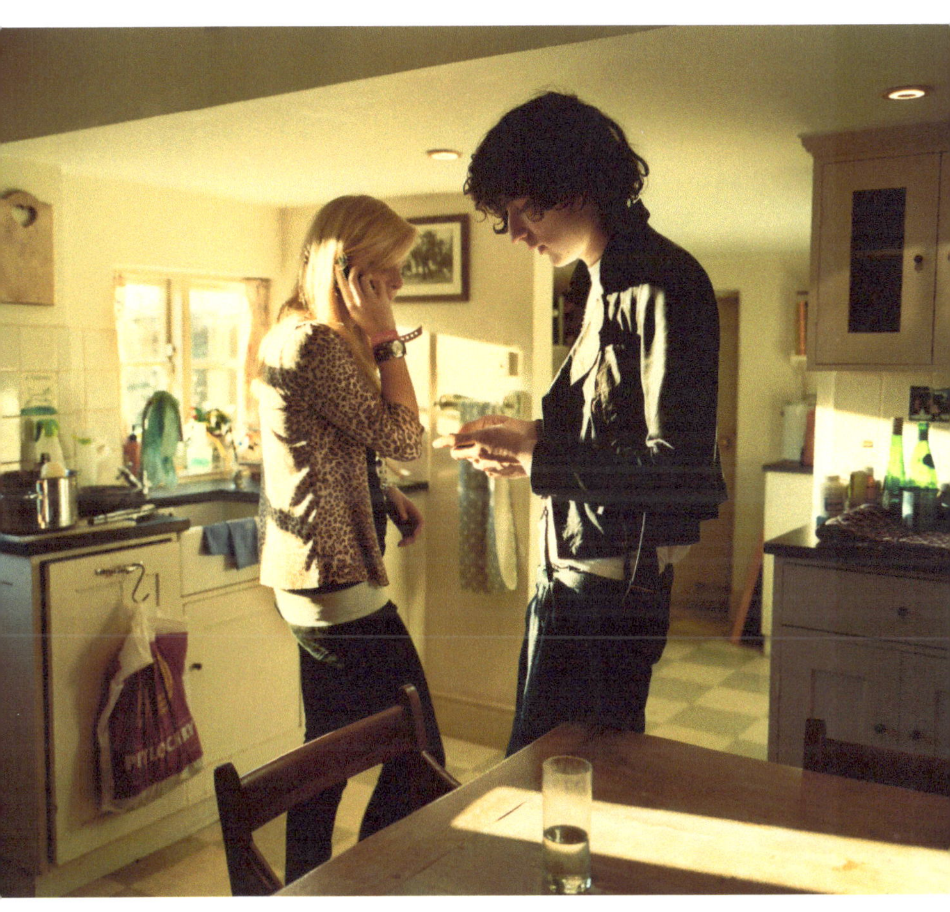

late spring/early evening in the kitchen

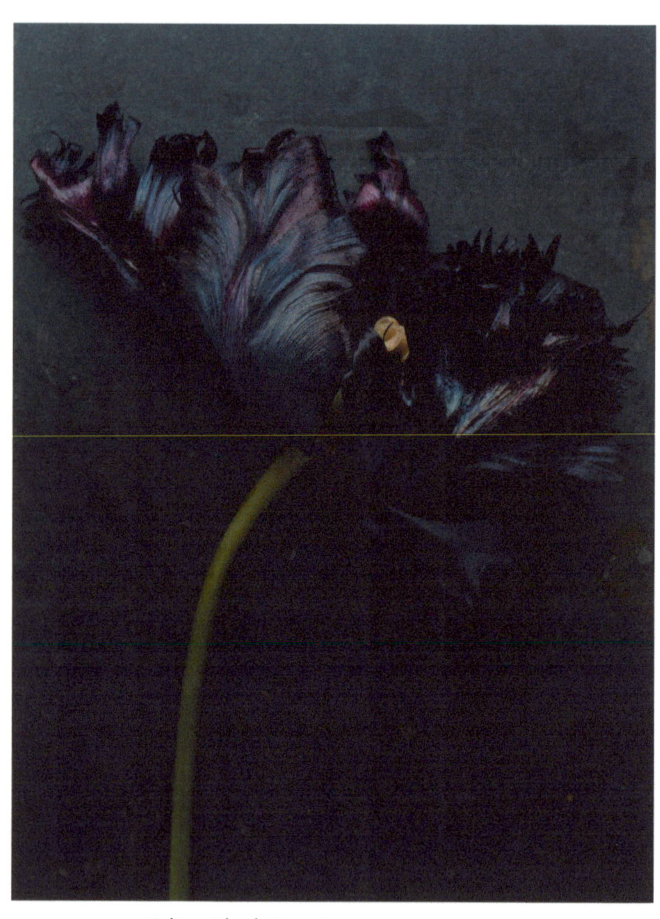

Tulipa Black Parrot

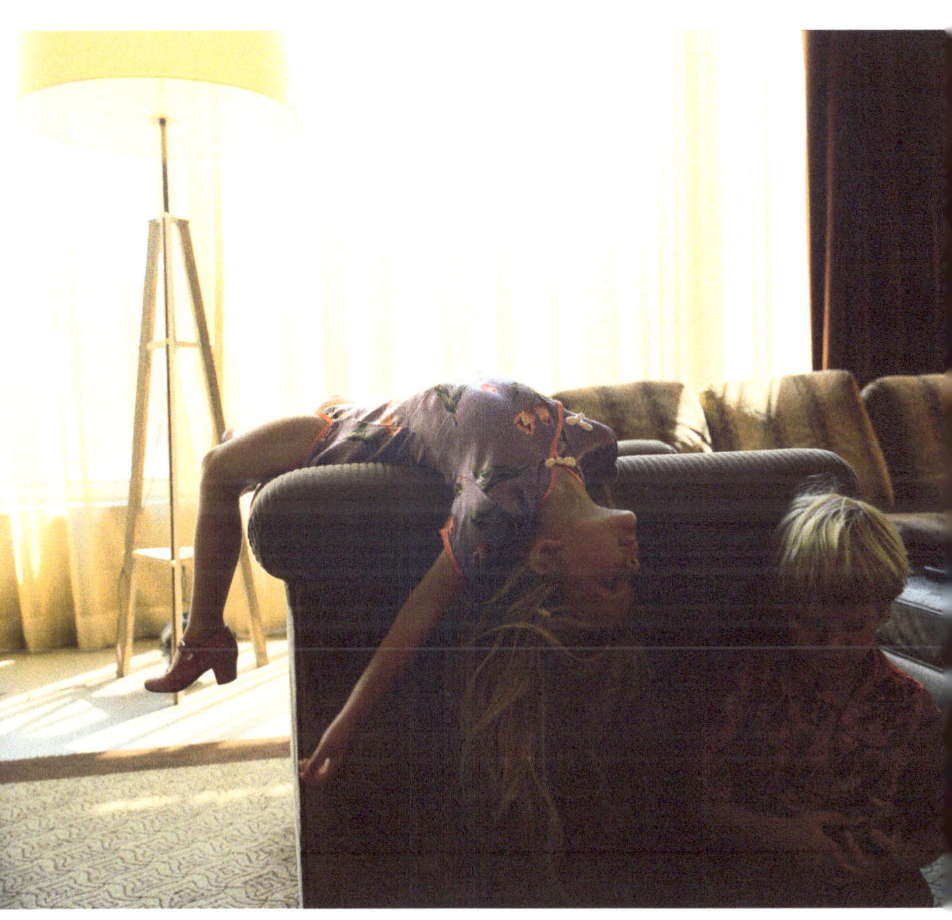

pokemon cards in a hotel lobby

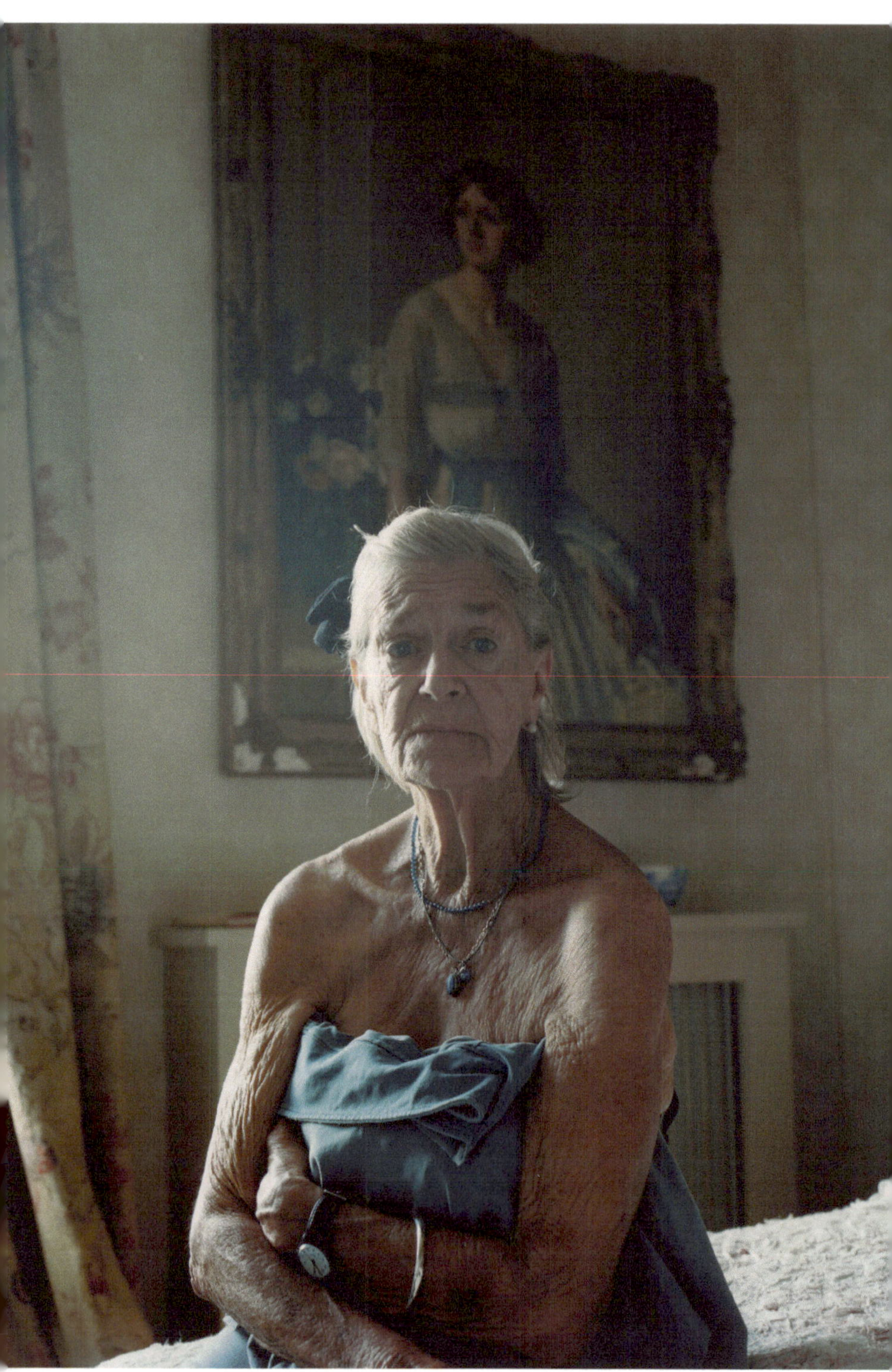

my mother and her mother

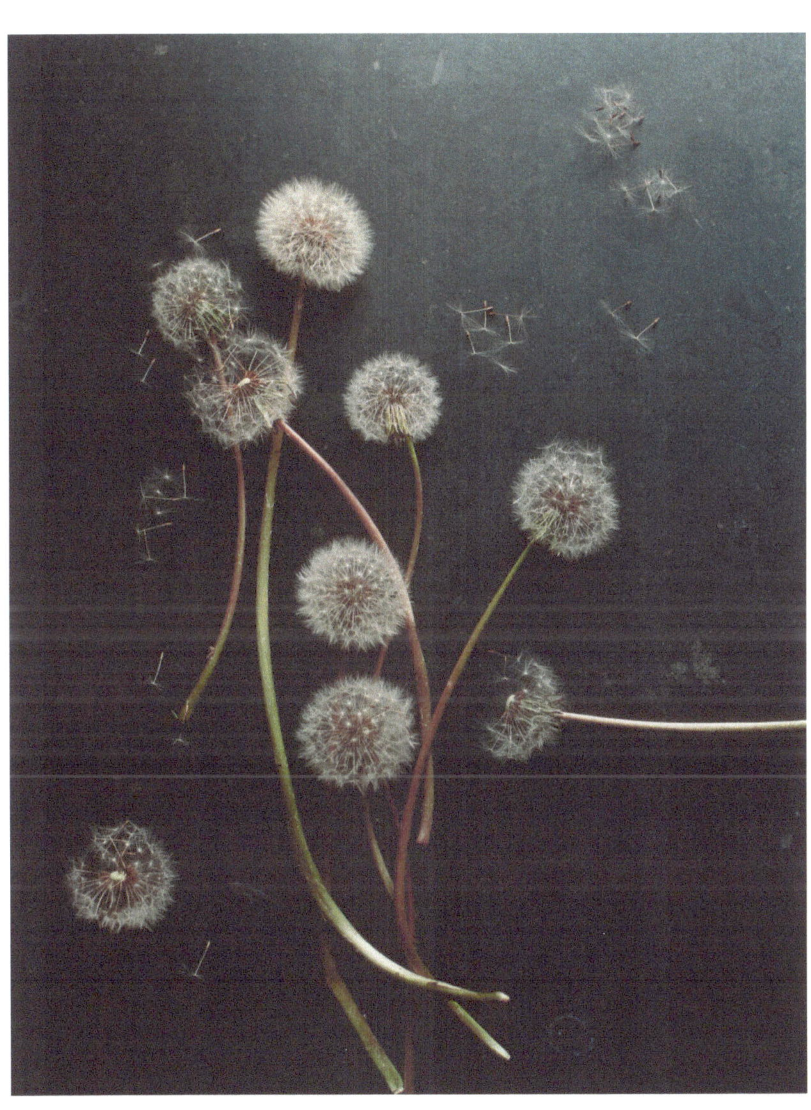

Taraxacum Officinale

Emma Hardy

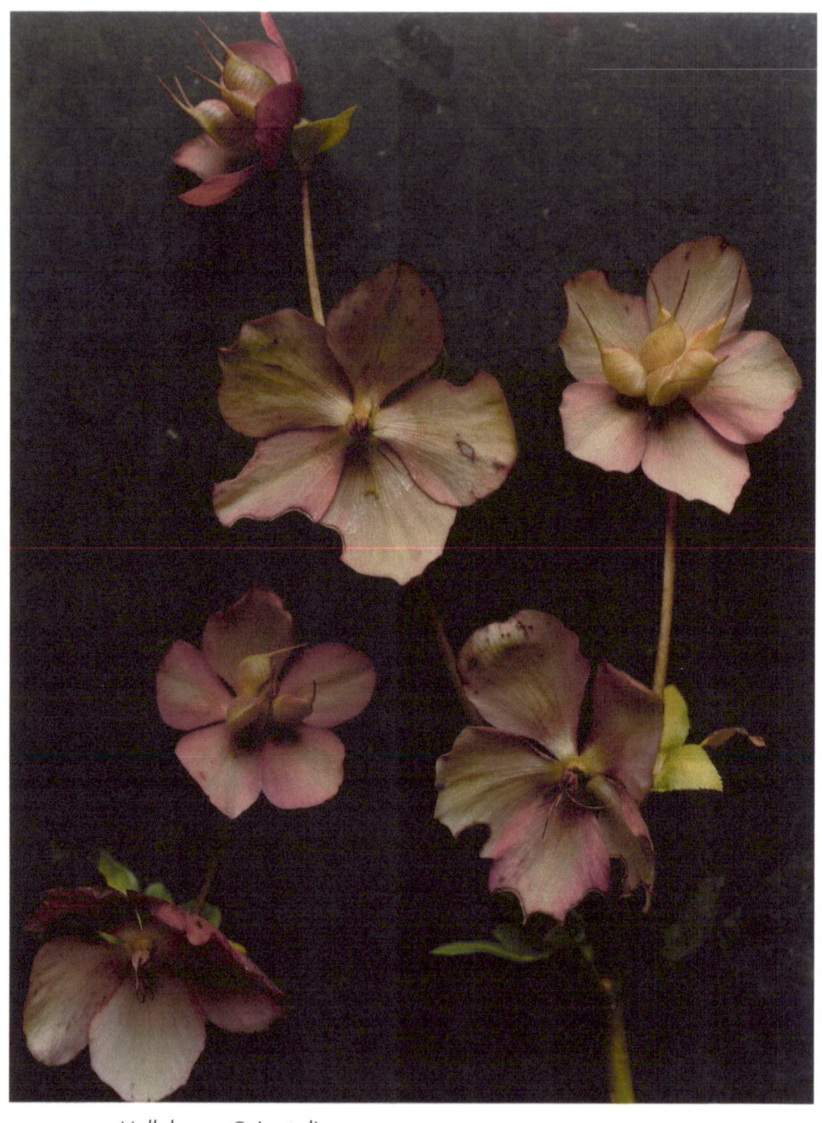

Helleborus Orientalis

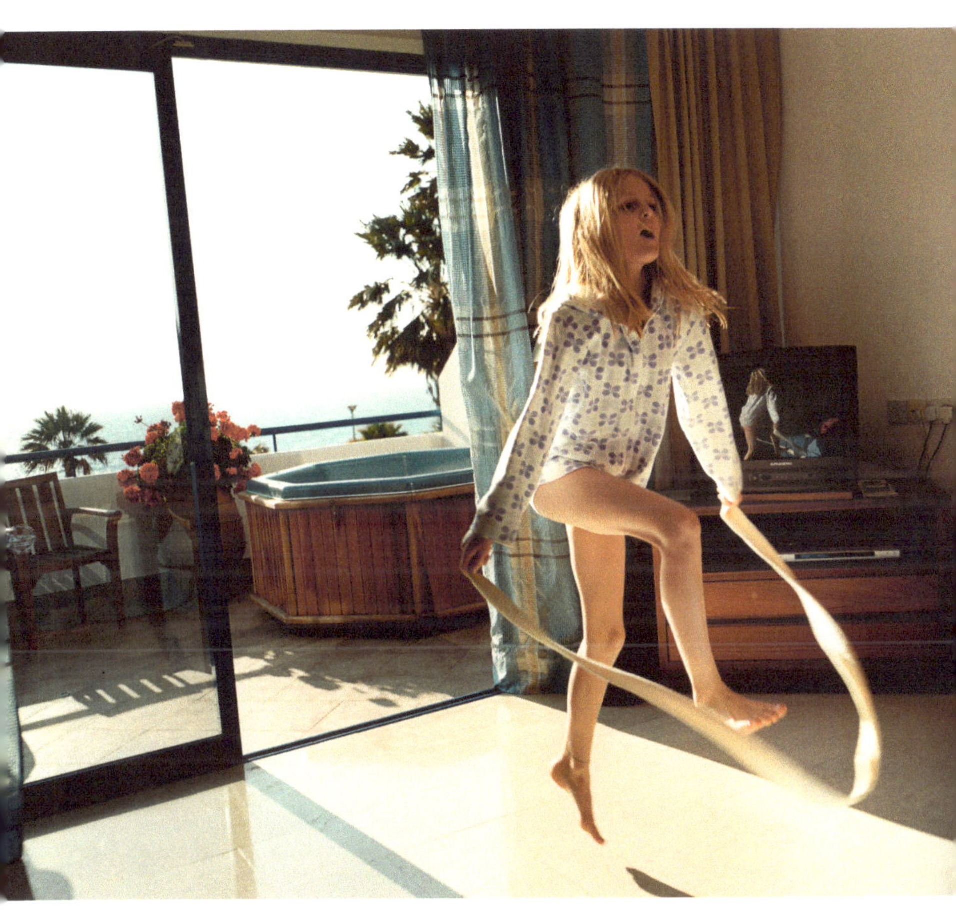

a hotel bathrobe belt

Tea and Testaments

Rituals abound but we're not having any
unless they're made instantly, in the rough,
on the fly, claimed as we trot through the rain,
searching for likely pre-made picnic sandwiches.
Pickles are a must, but do they go with rain?
To be at once artless and snide, one must be fifteen.
Sure, I play, blubby mother who's made up all the games,
but what goes with thunder?
Hot Peppers, of course. Anyone knows that.
Tricky, I dissemble, *because they clash terribly with lightning.*
Though, in truth, hot peppers go with anything at all.
She counts the seconds between booms and says
we have some time if we eat between the claps.
I knew she'd get her way.
And so sudden jars are added to our store
and icy bottles of sweet capricious tea
which are clinked, *salute*, in our humid car
as the sky defends itself from harm
and heat enflames the sea.

Previously published in *Mundane Joys: A Poetry Anthology* (Derailleur Press, 2021) and *As Above, So Below*, v. 1. 9 (2022).

Kate **Falvey**
b. 1958 USA

The Mothers

Howling will not do you any good.
There's work to be done, no use
being snooty about it.
Whoever rose from the dust, anyway?
Anyway, it's a lie if you've heard otherwise.
There are some flecks of old wisdom
winking in your rag. If you think
they are mouths you are mistaken, or,
maybe you're onto something. Mouths
of old mothers in the dust cloth. Why
not? when the Virgin (fat chance, that)
weeps toast tears into the scrambled eggs
or frowns unavailingly from a lichenous
daub of brick. The problem is
that you expect them to speak
and direct you when their voices are gagged
with your own desultory need. So
you end up having conversations with yourself.
And you still have to mop the shadows
from the parched, grief-maddened linoleum.

Previously published in *The Mom Egg* (2017).

DIY

She wonders if she pressed the book
into the nest of afghans and doilies
on purpose, with some notion of protecting
what it holds. Dozens of petals,
knit in shades of rose and lavender,
spill from the box – an unmade bed
quilt or some unrealized unstuffed creature
for one of the girls' rooms
when there were girls.

She remembers the bowl of wool upon
the coffee table she scavenged and tiled
in white and gold and bits of bitter blue
and the needles picking up light like stitches
dropped from the unruly, chiffon moon.
The babies were drunk from play and petulance,
flopped in flannel, dreaming of applesauce and earthworms.
She hears the girls flouncing in, flicking her with the
frilly trimmings of their small unravelings
and sees the threads of milk webbed in the honeyed tea
she brewed to calm their robust swirl of nerves.

She remembers suppers by candles that they dipped
together in the mist of aromatic, patient kitchen rites
and midnight purple layer cakes creamed
with impish green, scalloped jubilation,
and the paper cut out dolls flapping skirts—
their maniacal acrobatics, their tomboy legs
pleating against the leafy hand-hooked rug.

The book is plump with memory, snares and snippets
of their tangled pasts. And she recalls dressing the cover
with remnants from the clothing of her children—
the pinwale corduroys and finicky ginghams,
the toweling from cartooned baby bibs,
the communion serge and organdies,
the psychedelic lime and fuchsia stripes,
the chambray and the washed-fine denim
that straggled home with sighing grass stains late at night.

She smells the morning babies rubbing away their rest
and the oatmeal sticky on the mottled ivory of their cheeks.
She feels the pins pushed into the little apple cushion
and the thread pulled through another moonlit eye.

She eyes her new white muslin needlepoint,
blowzy and reluctant in its patient ancient hoop,
sprigged with green points of departure
in an effrontery of blankness.

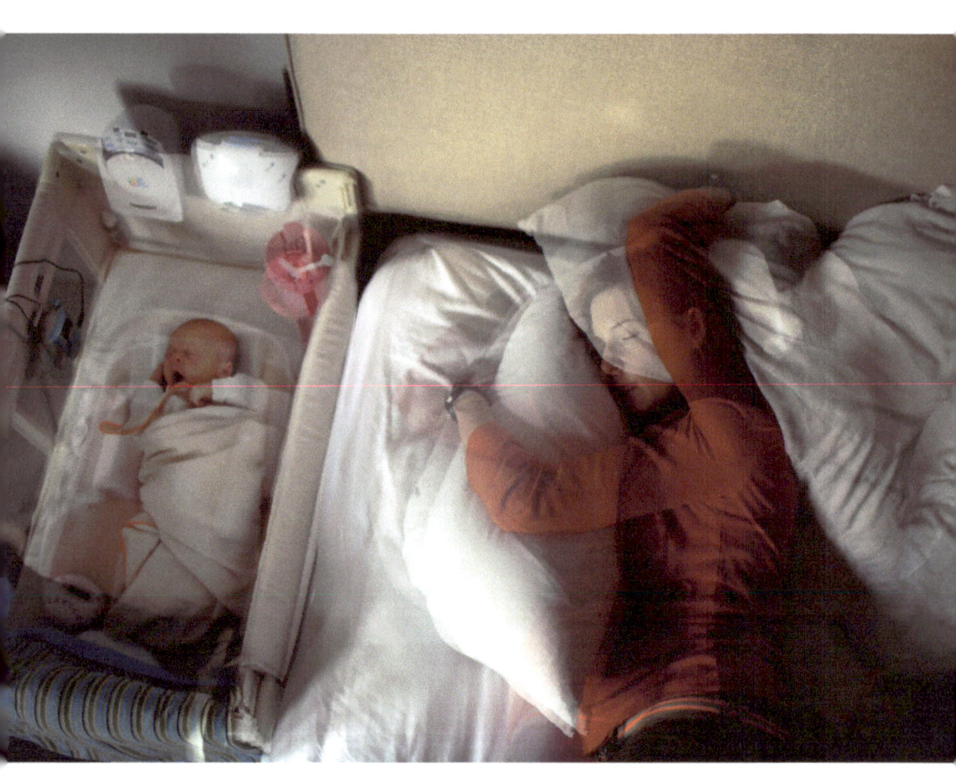

The Day the Baby Ended Up in the Emergency Room (2007 / 2021)
Archival Pigment Print, 13 x 20 inches / 33 x 51 cm, Edition of 5

Tabitha **Soren**

b. 1967 USA

Motherload

2021

"This project began as a hedge against life as a mother overtaking life as an artist," writes Tabitha Soren. To create her series *Motherload*, shot over 2006-07 and then later conceived and printed in 2021, she suspended a camera above her bed to capture the first three months of newborn life. She then layered multitudes of images atop each other, illustrating the haze of repetitive gestures and slight movements that comprise so much of post-partum life. Time blurs. It stops. It never stops.

Motherload is an cumulative experience, with its dizzying sameness conveying both the monotonous reality of intimate caregiving as well as the irreplaceable potency of magic that blinks into existence for just one moment... and then blinks again, gone.

tabithasoren.com

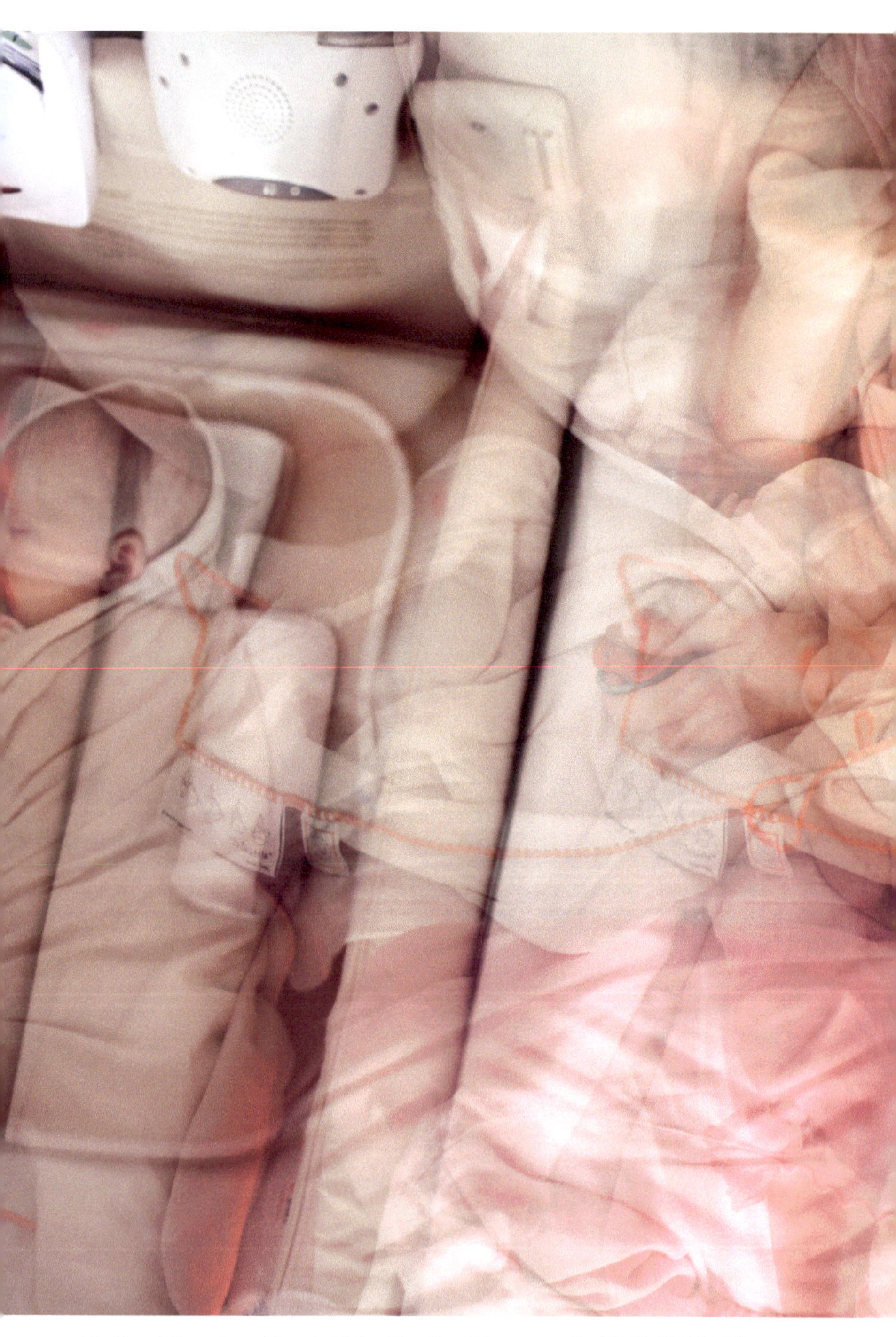

My Great American Novel, All the Daytime Photographs (2006-07 / 2021)
Archival Pigment Print, 13 x 20 inches / 33 x 51 cm, Edition of 5

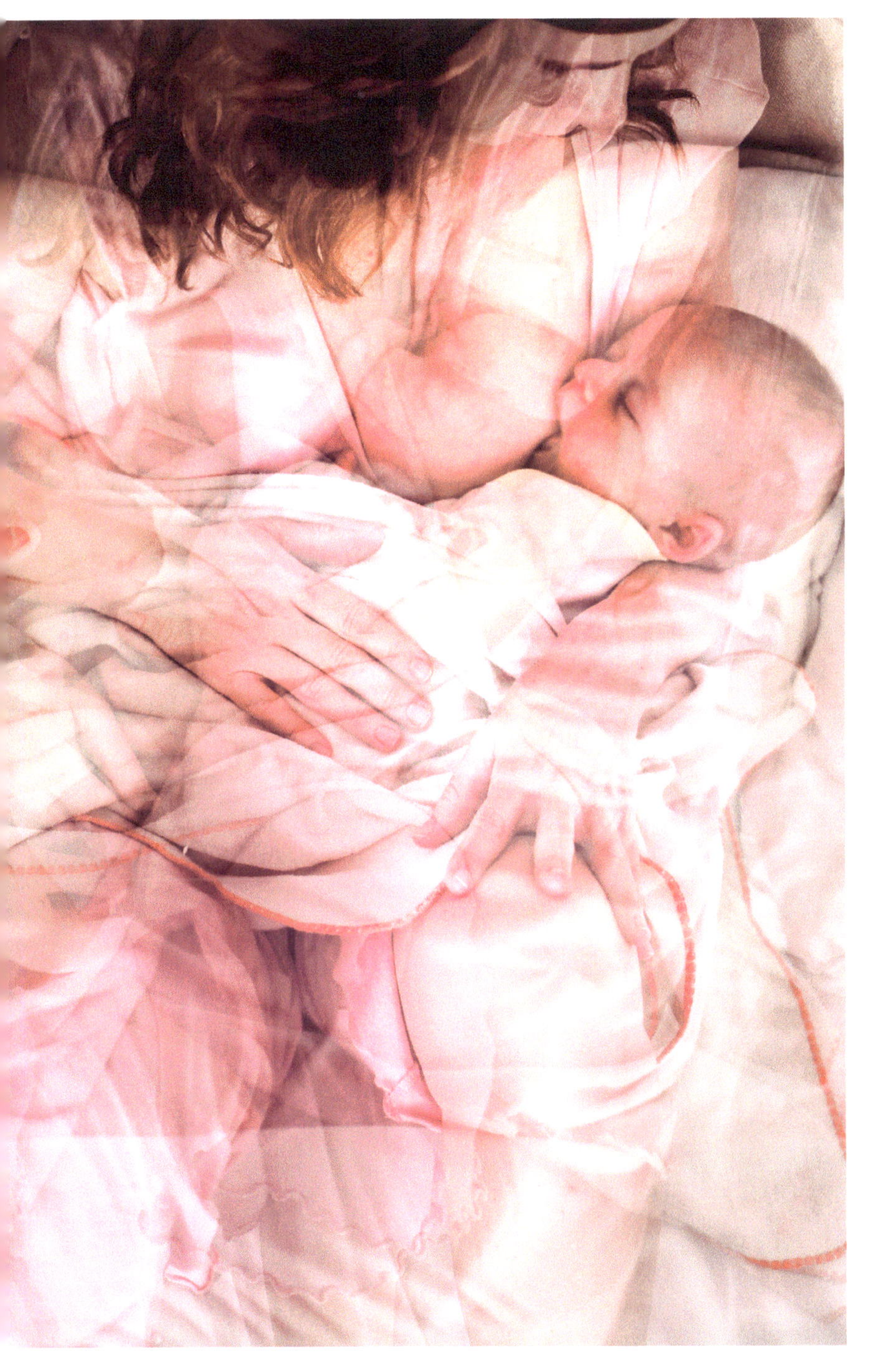

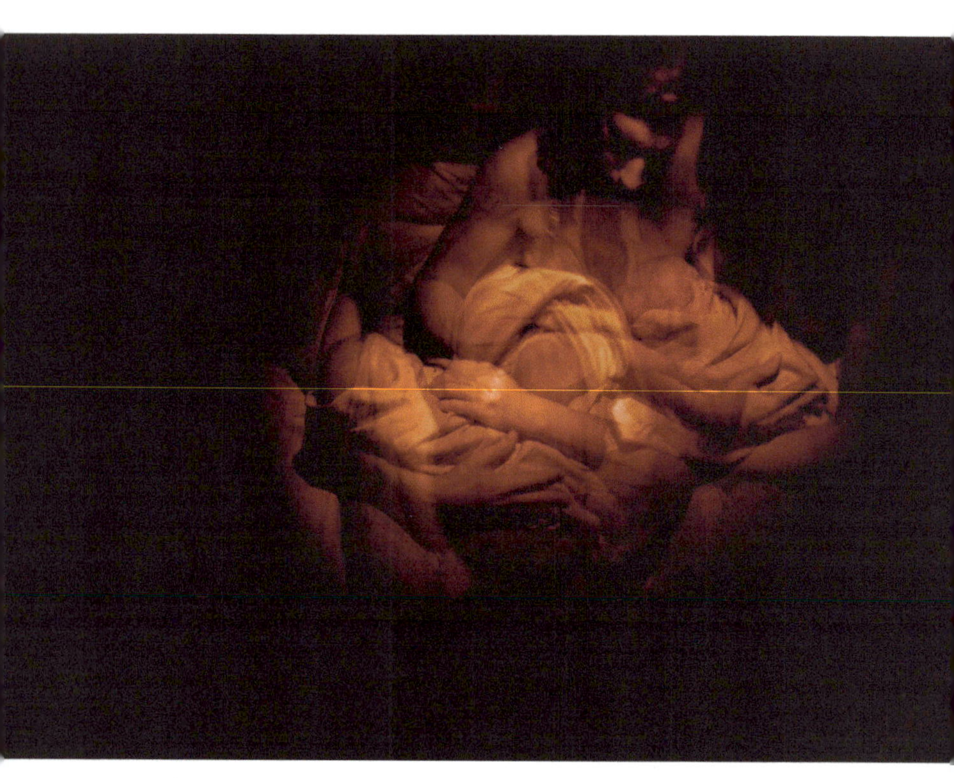

The Month He Ended up in the Emergency Room (2007 / 2021)
Archival Pigment Print, 13 x 20 inches / 33 x 51 cm, Edition of 5

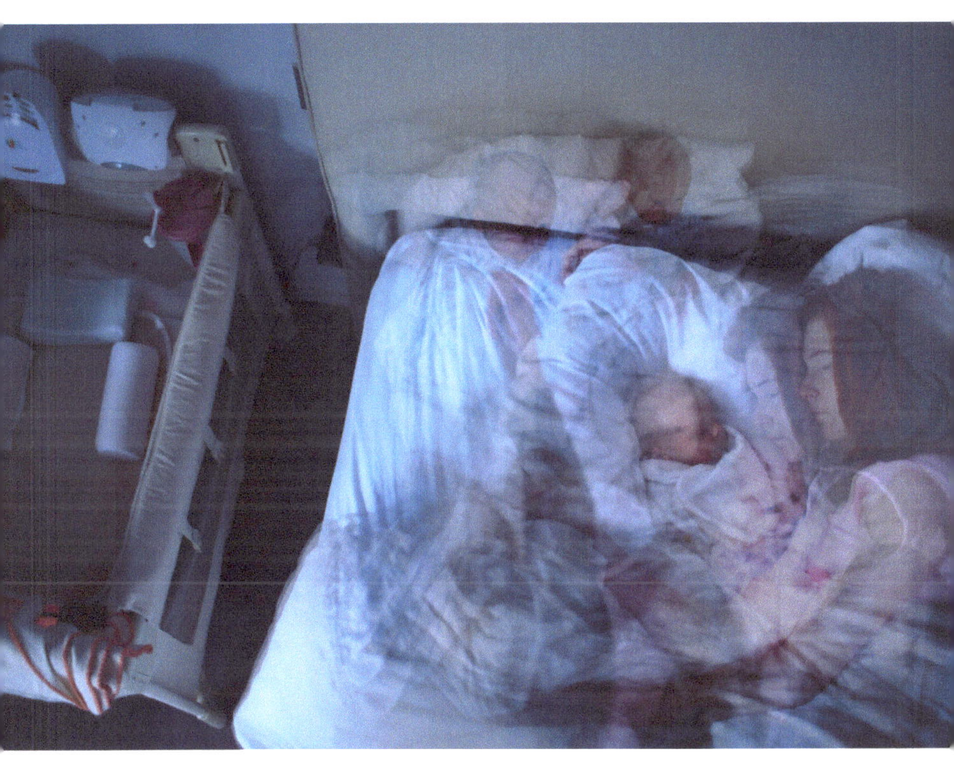

The Night the Baby Only Woke Up Twice (2007 / 2021)
Archival Pigment Print, 13 x 20 inches / 33 x 51 cm, Edition of 5

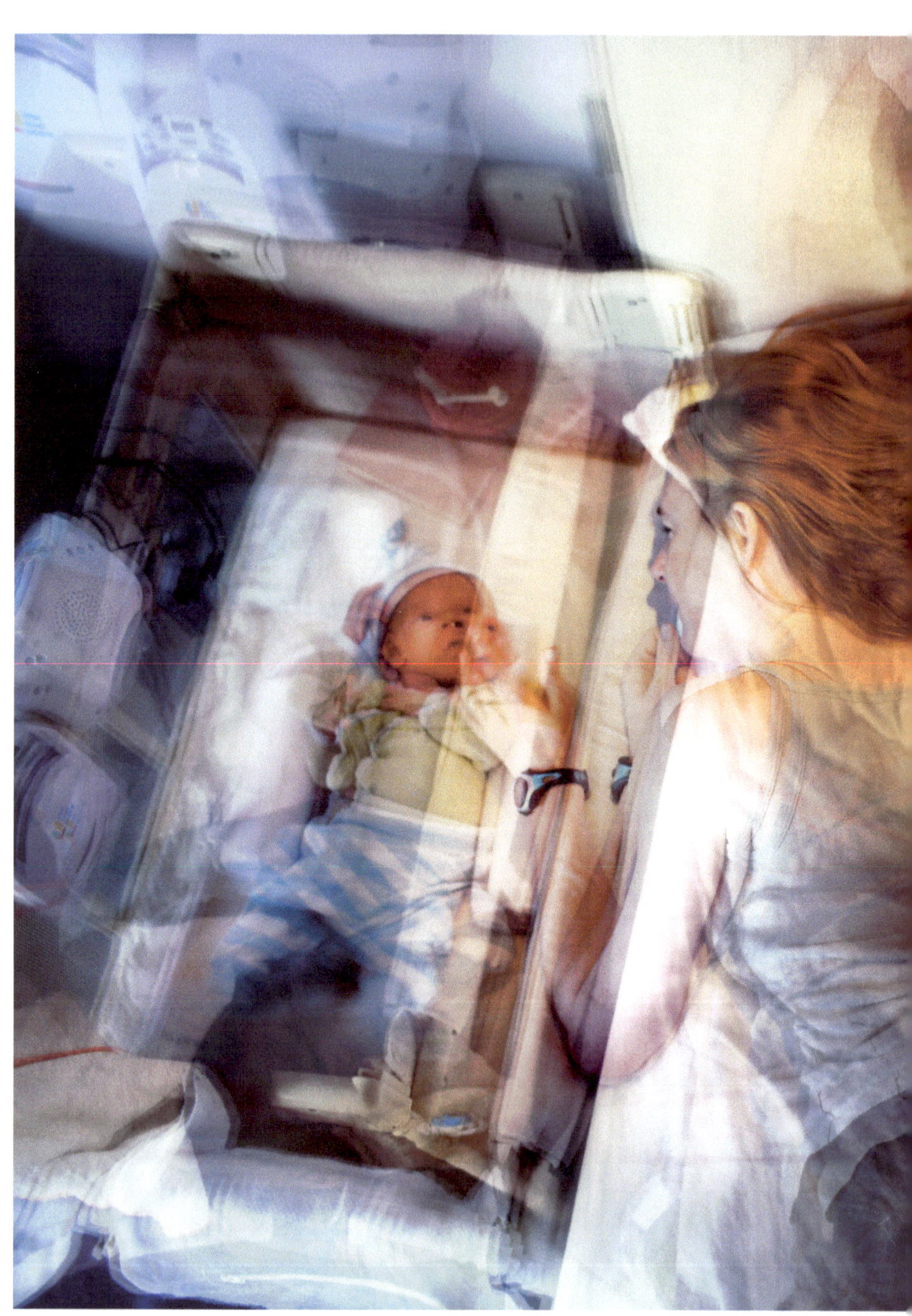

The Month I Could Walk Without Peeing on Myself (2007 / 2021)
Archival Pigment Print, 13 x 20 inches / 33 x 51 cm, Edition of 5

Tabitha Soren

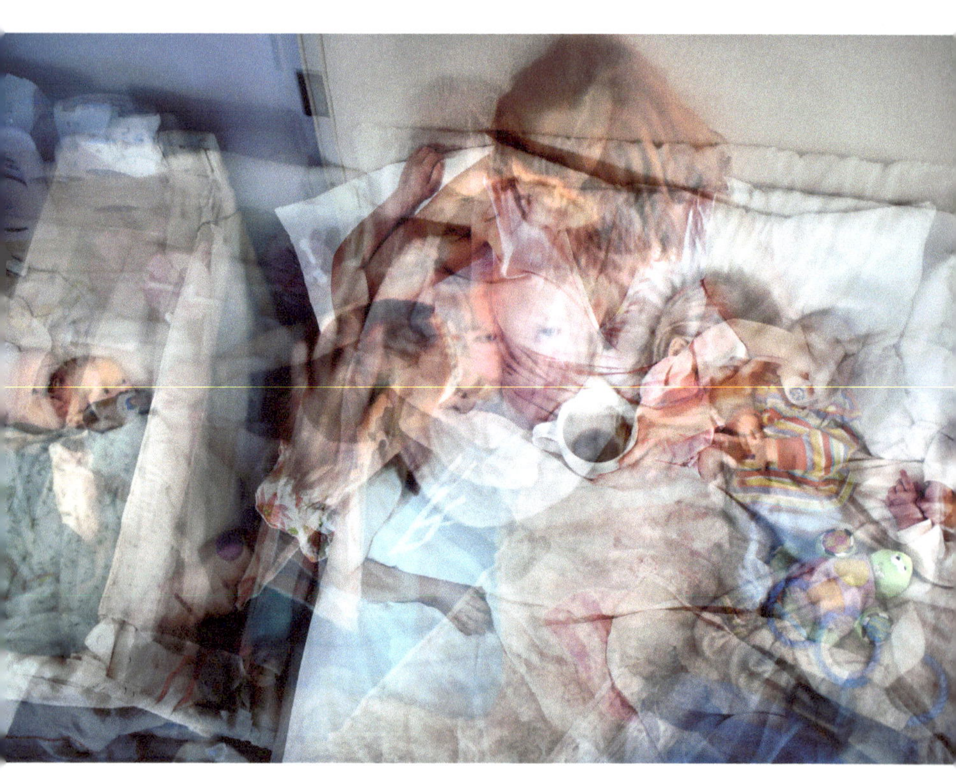

Running with Weights On (2007 / 2021)
Archival Pigment Print, 13 x 20 inches / 33 x 51 cm, Edition of 5

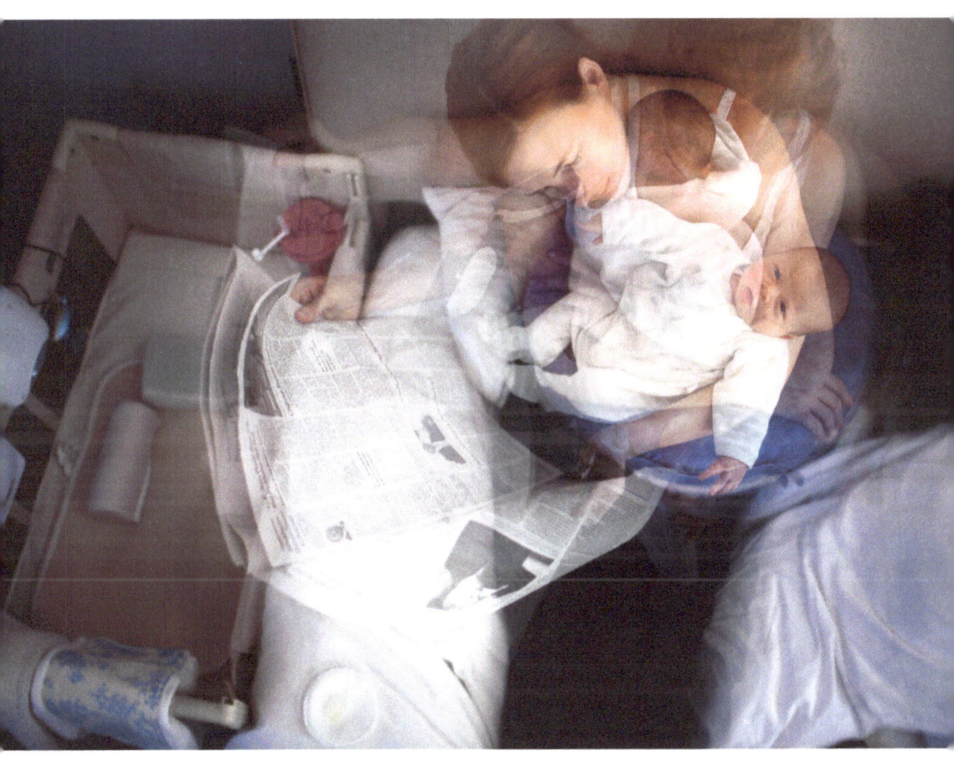

The Day After the Baby Slept Through the Night (2007 / 2021)
Archival Pigment Print, 13 x 20 inches / 33 x 51 cm, Edition of 5

Tabitha Soren

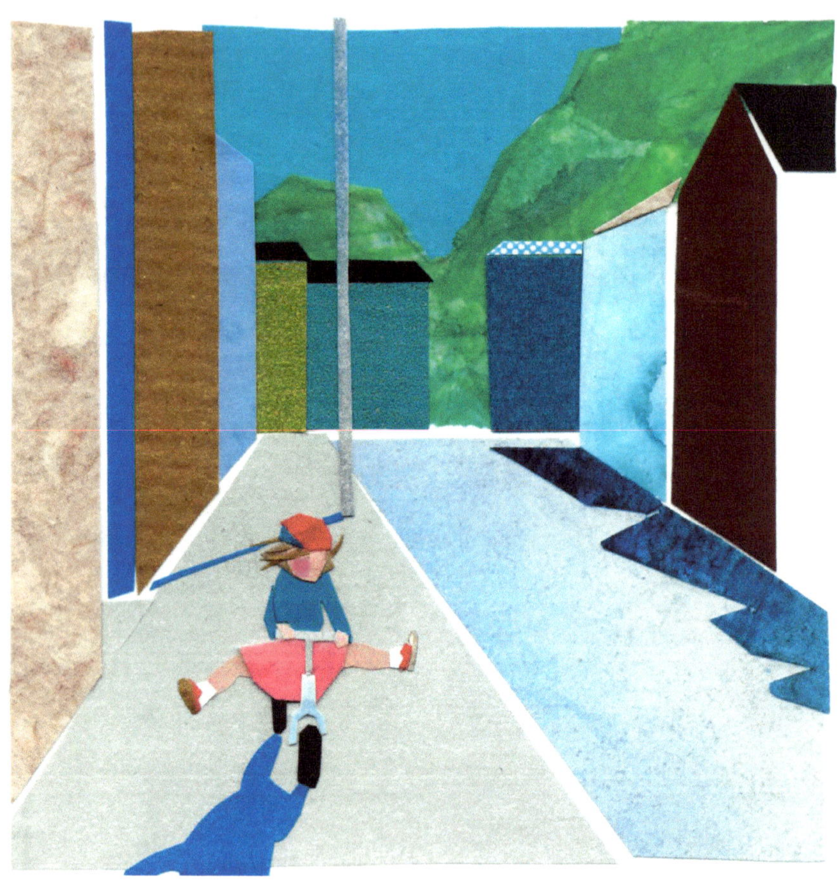

Elena Skoreyko Wagner
b. 1984 Canada

100 Days of Lidi Pie
2018 - ongoing

"Parenting young children is really just normal life with an extreme and often absurd focus on the most visceral, frustrating and mundane aspects," Elena Skoreyko Wagner writes. "There were beautiful bits, but I found they were often lost under the laundry heap." In need of both an outlet and a means of giving more attention to the everyday magic under her nose, she committed herself to making 100 cut paper collages of life with her daughter Alida, or Lidi Pie. The result was an evolving chronicle of, as she says, "The funny, weird, beautiful, wise, unexpected, heart-wrenching magic a small child keeps in their pocket and shares almost exclusively with you."

Deep in the throes of parenting a toddler and a preschooler, Skoreyko Wagner had to make do with 20-minute intervals, working on her lap or the corner of the kitchen table. "I kept a little baggie of snippets, a glue stick and small pair of scissors in a small box, and would carry it from room to room, ready to work on it in the margins of life." Making the artworks, portably sized at 12 x 12 cm, allowed her to transcend the daily slog and focus instead on the more sparkly bits of having a toddler. Skoreyko Wagner is now approaching the end of her series, but finds that she's dragging out the final collages, not yet ready to let go of her celebration of mothering joys with Lidi Pie.

elenastreehouse.com

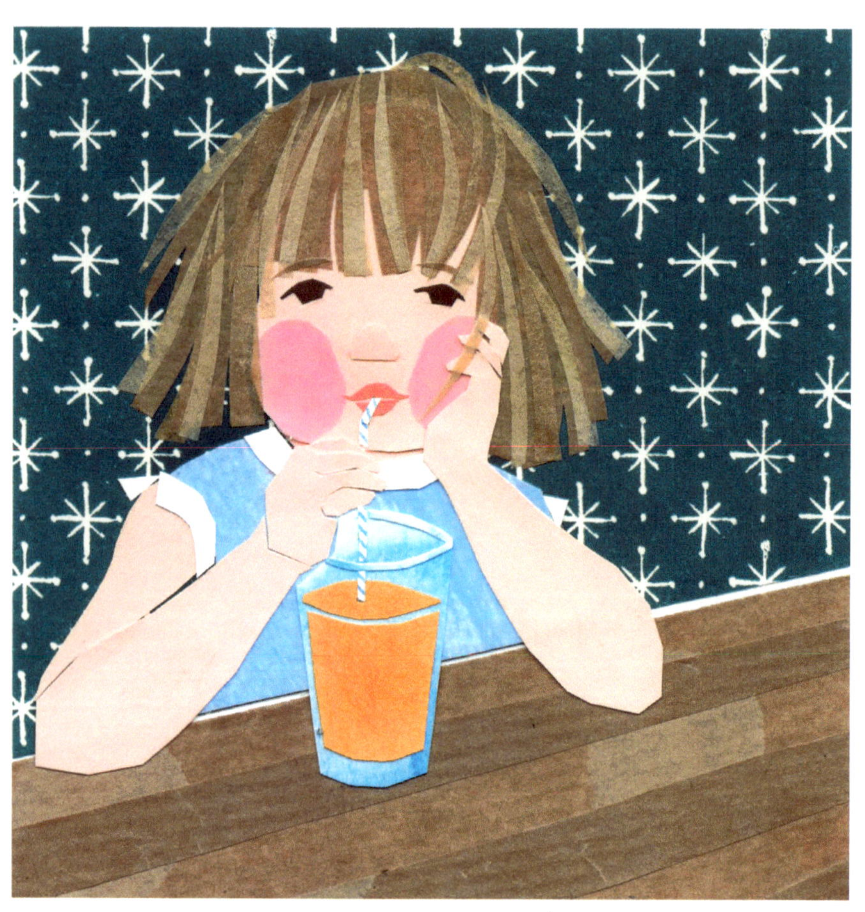

"If everyone in the world shares, then I will call it Happy World. Not England."

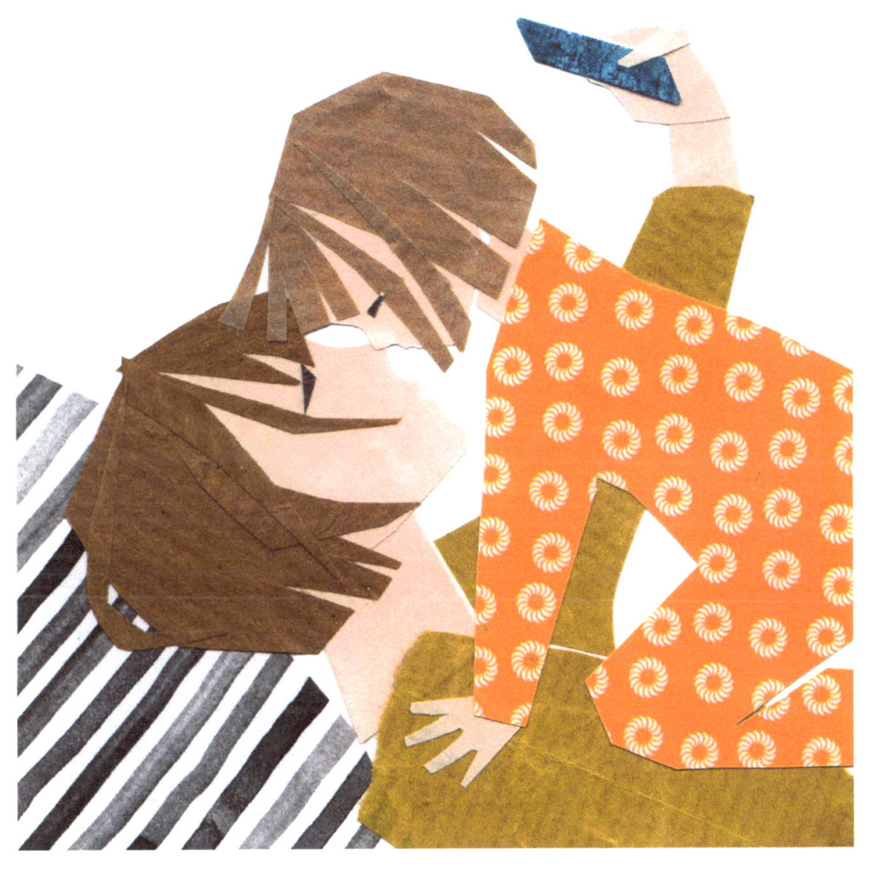

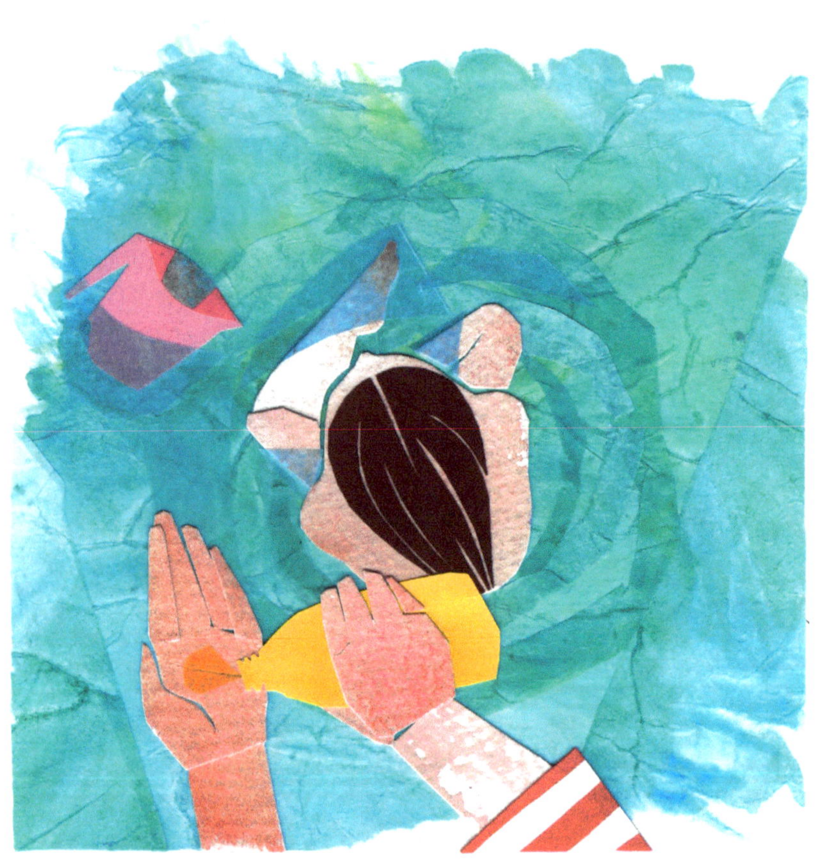

Lidi Pie: "Ahh!! THERE'S SOAP IN MY NOSE!!"
Me: "What!? How could that be? I just put it on your head!"
She wails inconsolably.
Me: "Lidi. I think you are just smelling it."
Lidi Pie: "Oh."

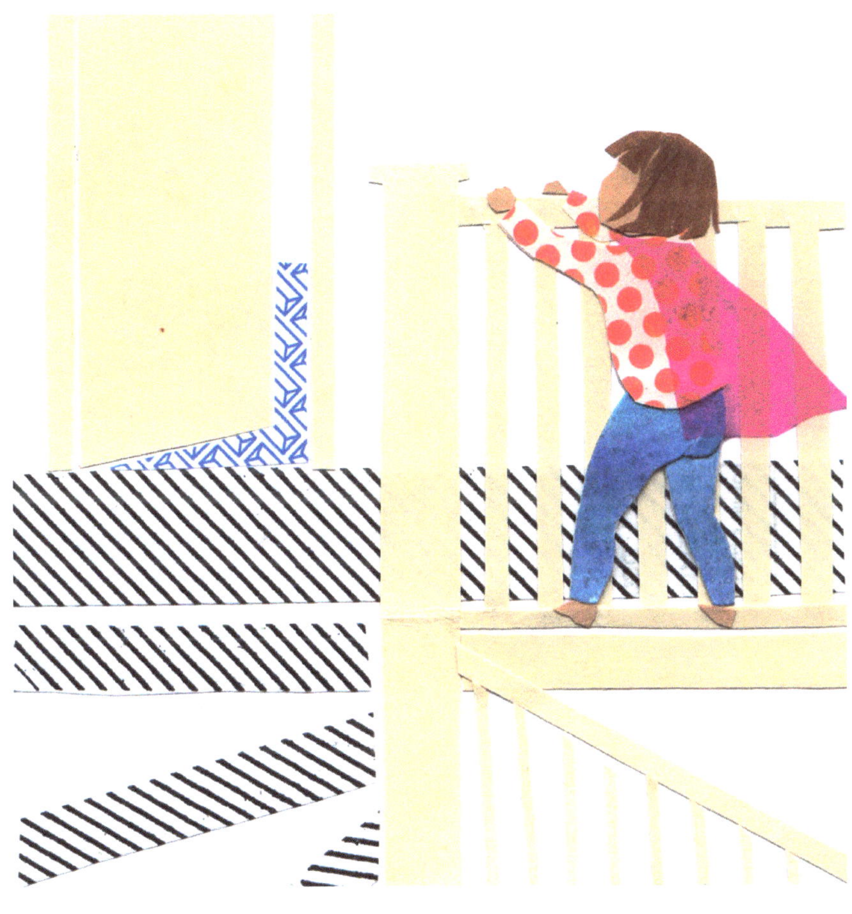

"I love dees jeans! They're so snuggly and great!
Dey make me like a superhero!"

Elena Skoreyko Wagner

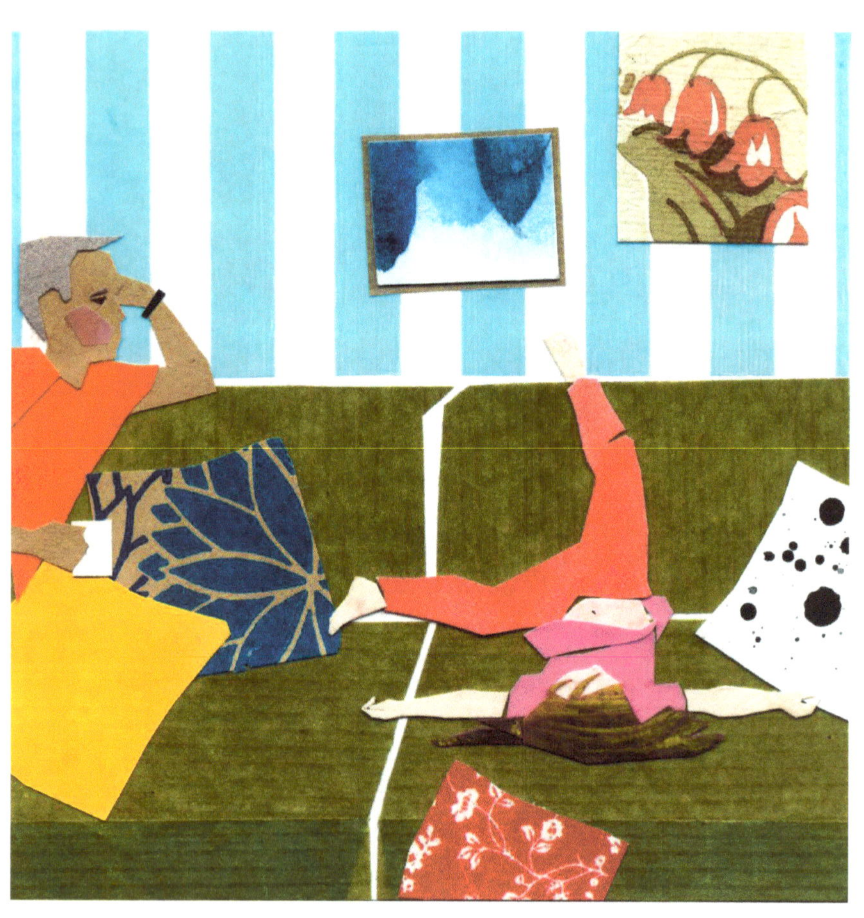

"You're not me, I'm me"

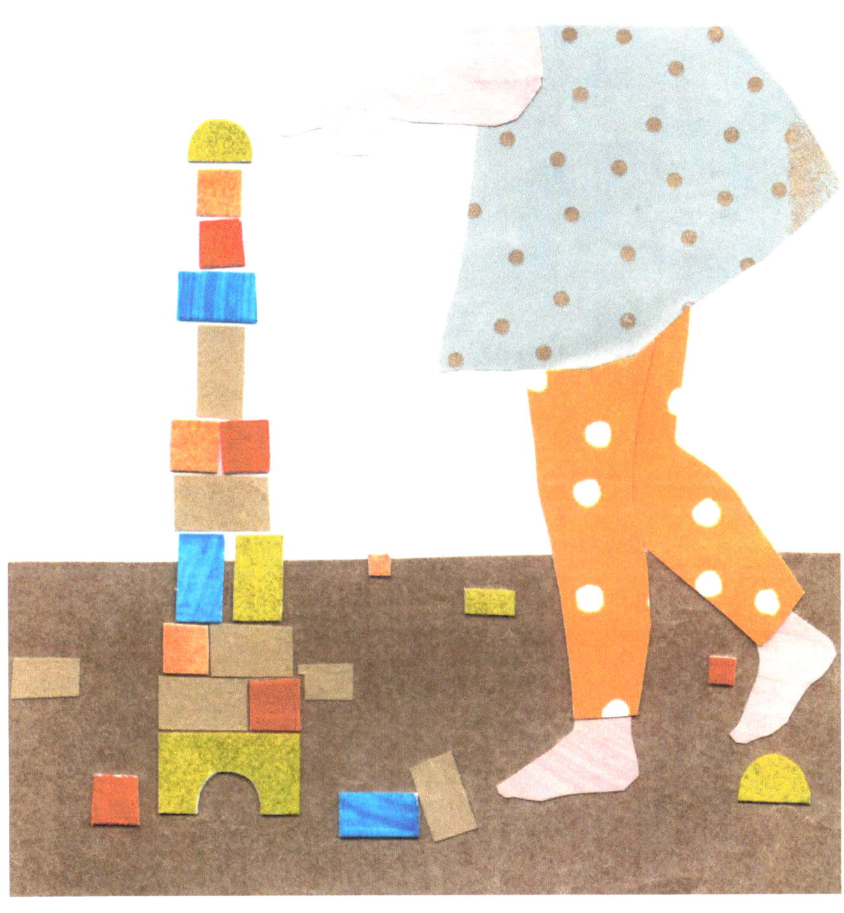

"Just a li'l boop"

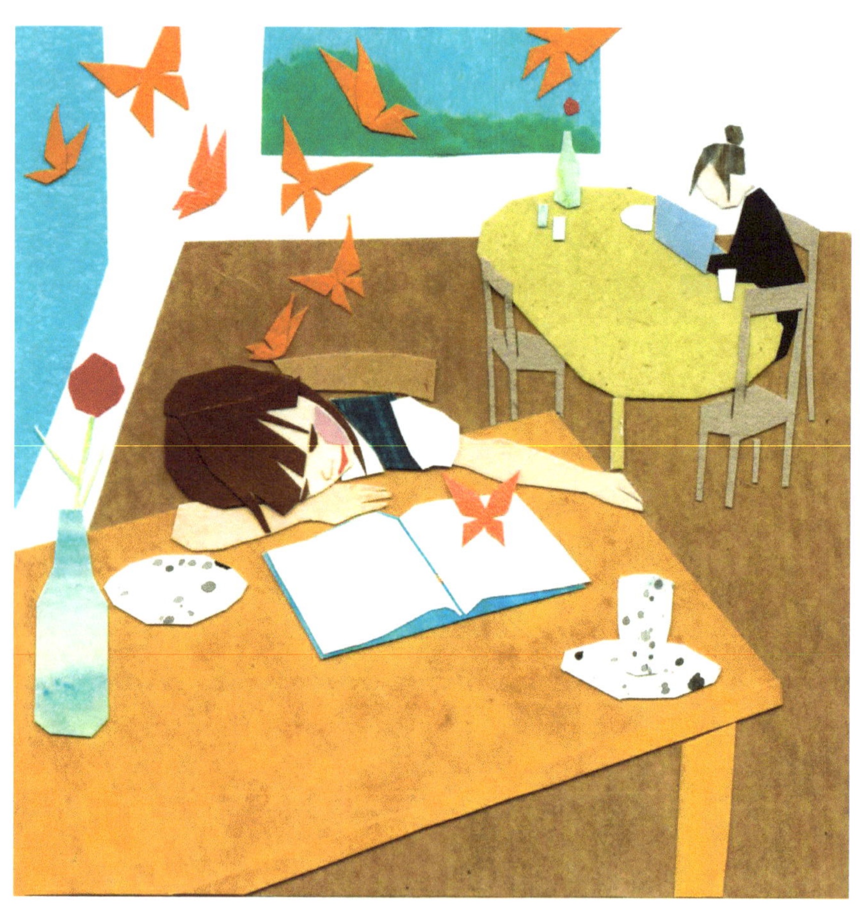

"If there was one hundred and fifty butterflies inside here, the whole house would fly."

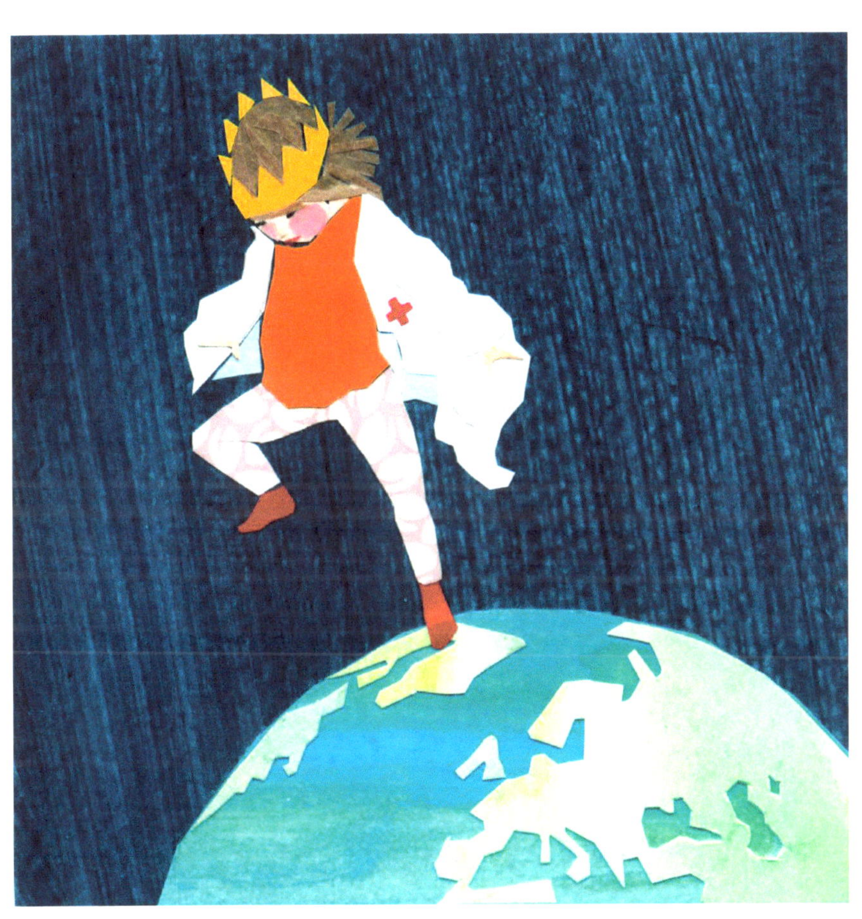

"Look, look Jonah! You've never seen dis before! I open my doctor jacket and -- dah da dahhhh! I'm a princess too."

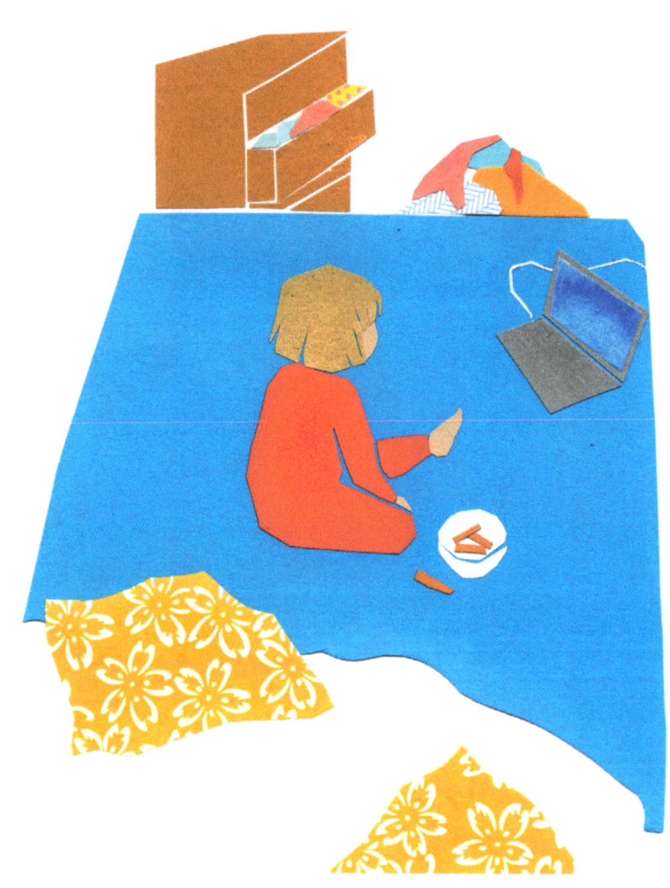

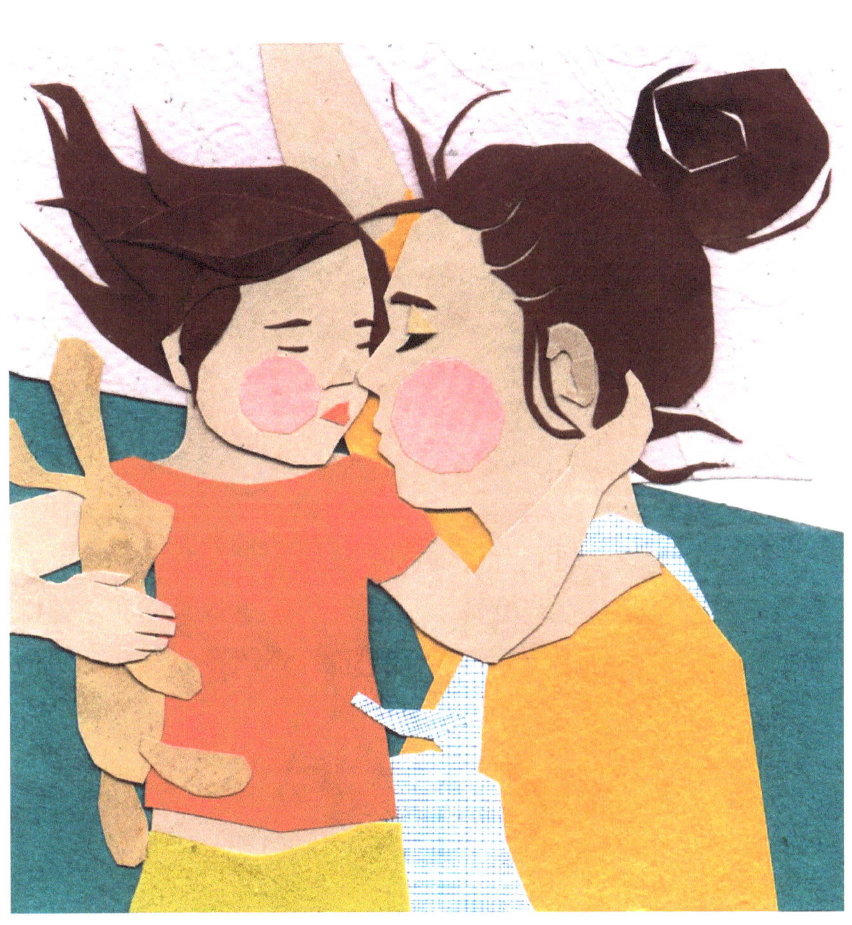

"Who am I when I am not your spoon?"

Elena Skoreyko Wagner

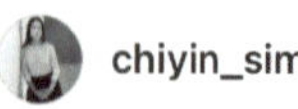

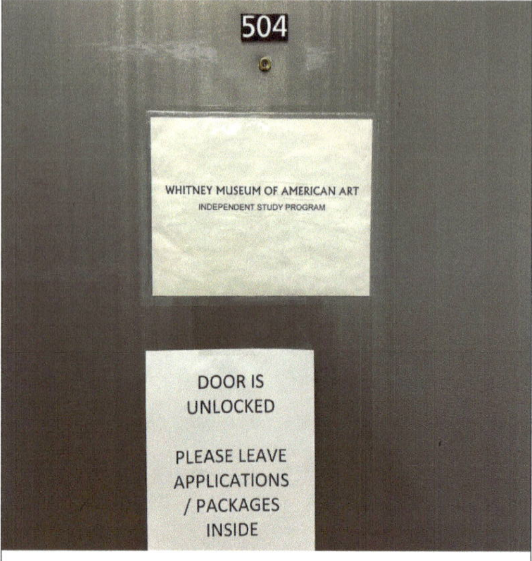

 Liked by **264 others**

chiyin_sim "Mama, where is your school?" / "It's in Manhattan. But it runs late and mama will likely get home after your bedtime." / "Why?" — conversations with Lucas Yiwei, 2 years and 5 months. | Excited to join the Whitney Independent Study Programme (studio track) this academic year, in a cohort of interesting artists, curators and critical writers/ scholars. I may be the grandma of the group but it's my third career and there's much to learn and explore. It is a special juncture for the long-running programme in this form, but perhaps the start of a new chapter of making, thinking and doing for many of us. Onward! #whitneyisp #artistmum #artistparent

View all 10 comments

21 September 2022

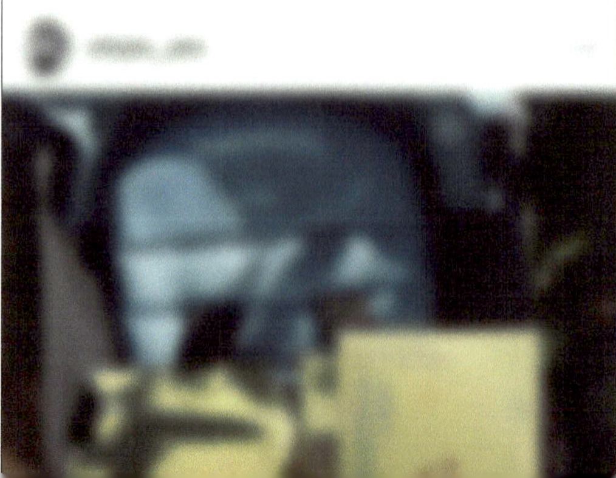

Sim Chi Yin

b. 1978 Singapore

Sim Chi Yin is an artist whose long career trajectory has taken her from documentary photography and filmmaking into complex transmedia works. With an extensive list of publications, grants, residencies, and solo exhibitions under her belt, she recently also became a mother.

Over the last couple of years, she began posting openly about her child and some of the challenges of being an artist-mother. She speaks in this interview about making her experience public, the working artist's lifestyle of travel and relocation with a small child, and the added costs of doing business when it comes to childcare.

You post on a regular basis about being a mom: from photos of your son's stroller filled with copies of your photobook, to asking questions about including the cost of childcare in a grant application. A lot of artists still don't say *anything* about it, to the extent that you wouldn't even know that they're mothers. So, let's just start with asking: Why?

Isn't it shocking, though, that this is *still* happening in this day and age, and in our generation? I've come across some literature from a conference in the 1980s, where a bunch of artist-mothers got together to discuss this, and they did a survey and concluded that most try to hide the fact that they have kids. I wasn't very conscious of this when I first started to share these things, but now I'm pretty determined to do the radical opposite. I don't *want* to hide it. There's lots of reasons why people would choose to, but I am experimenting with the radical opposite of hiding.

How did the 'radical opposite' get started, if not consciously?
It's just one of the biggest pieces of my life right now. If I'm going to be honest about my life then it has to be present. Maybe initially it was a way to find support and solidarity. I'm not networked among the artist-mother circles yet, plus we've moved base three times in the last two years, so I'm also not really networked *physically* with any kind of group. So, I just kind of put it out there.

Again, I know there's lots of reasons that people have to hide it – there's a lot of assumptions that come from being a parent of a young child. I think people naturally assume that you're not going to be nearly as serious about your work, you're not going to be reliable, you're not going to be able to pull off a big solo show or a new commission, you can't hang out and party late into the night, you can't go to openings. But I actually signed on to my second gallery when I was in my final months of pregnancy, so that was a pleasant bit of support.

They knew you were pregnant?
Oh, yeah! I went to the interview pregnant. I flew in to Berlin to meet with the gallerist right at the end of my second trimester, so if they'd wanted to meet any later, I wouldn't have been able to fly.

I've also had the other end of the spectrum, with people making comments about how I'm going to start making work that's all about babies, so it's a mixed bag. There were some very sexist comments, for sure. People do assume that you will be less reliable and you will have less time to work, therefore your work be less good. After the birth,I took a sabbatical of a year, and then when I came back to work, I put myself forward at an agency and there were murmurs, like, "Oh, her work is no good ever since she had a child." It's fine. In that particular case, I think there were some very specific circumstances that I won't go into here. There had been a shift in my work and it didn't fit with the existing group, so it was better to part ways.

What has been your response?
In the art world, as well as in academia, you still hear assumptions made about parents, and I don't know what else to do but to be radically open about the fact that I do have a child. He is young, he needs my attention, but I am also working full-fledge on multiple things all the time. It is a fact that my time is more sliced and diced in multiple ways. It's true that I can't hang out every night of the week.

When I was young and commitment-free, I could hang out—there's a sense that time is infinite. Whereas now, it's a zero-sum game between very urgent choices.

However, I've continued to produce new work and I've continued to have shows. It just means I have to work ever harder. It does come with a lot of coordination with my partner because he has a full-on career himself, too. We're both crazily overcommitted professionally, we both have books coming out, and we both have multiple fires burning at the same time, and on top of that, we have to keep our son alive and happy. It's definitely a very difficult thing. But we just have to figure it out, right?

At this point, our interview is interrupted when Chi Yin sees on her baby monitor that Lucas, who was ill with a cold, has vomited in his room, and rushes to him. We continue around 15 minutes later.

I want to come back to what you said about people expecting you to start making work about babies, because, on one hand, that's indeed a sexist assumption. On the other hand, is it not also sexist to dismiss it as a lesser art? Would it be so bad to make art about babies?
I don't think it's bad, I just think it's a throwaway thing that people like to say. Since I'm mainly a photo artist, suddenly everyone says I'm going to start making pictures like Anne Geddes. It's just a stereotype people have, and that's what is dismissing.

I've seen many, many good pieces of art about motherhood, like Mary Kelly's work "Post-partum Document." That's a seminal work all about motherhood. And recently, I've seen a couple of amazing contemporary art shows that were created by new mothers—one

"Motherhood got me thinking
about the possibilities of repair
and restitution, the future,
rather than being totally
focused on past and trauma."

From "The Suitcase Is A Little Bit Rotten", courtesy Autograph London and the artist.

was Ani Liu and another Ghislaine Leung. Then there's this group called Designing Motherhood here in the US, who just curated an entire show in Boston on artist-mothers. I'm not part of this conversation yet, but it's heartening to see the conversation is really active.

I became quite self-conscious of *not* making work about motherhood for a while, until it made sense for Lucas Yiwei, my son, to start appearing in the work. I got a new commission from Autograph London, and over time and discussions with the curators, the work became not about motherhood per se but about transgenerational inheritance and memory. So, in that context it made sense and that's the first time he's appeared in my work. I've been dealing with my family history, and increasingly, I felt that the past also needs somewhere to go. It just came about naturally, since he is the next chapter of this 'history in the making,' and it made sense to think about the link between him and his great-grandfather, who had been written out of the family history – and whose Chinese name I gave him.

I guess I feel a bit guilty that I haven't even photographed Lucas or our family with, like, a 'real camera.' I've only made a bunch of phone photographs. I felt very envious when I saw both Ani Liu's and Ghislane Leung's work recently because I thought, "Wow, this is *everything*." I could relate to all of it. These artists are so clever. They've parlayed their mothering into amazing art projects. But it hasn't come naturally to me to make work about mothering head-on, so I'm coming into it with the angle of transgenerational inheritance.

How has becoming a mother changed your work?
I wouldn't say that *becoming a mother* is what shifted the plates for me exactly. I mean, I moved away from photography a few years ago because I became more interested in other forms and the work itself was taking me to other ways of storytelling. I'm still doing work that often begins from photography, but ends up being filmic, or a book, a performance, writing and scripting—things like that.

If anything, I suppose motherhood has made me think about those transgenerational questions a lot more. In the new work, I'm looking at not just what transpires across the generations, but the idea of what's already inscribed on a new human being coming into the

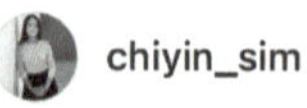

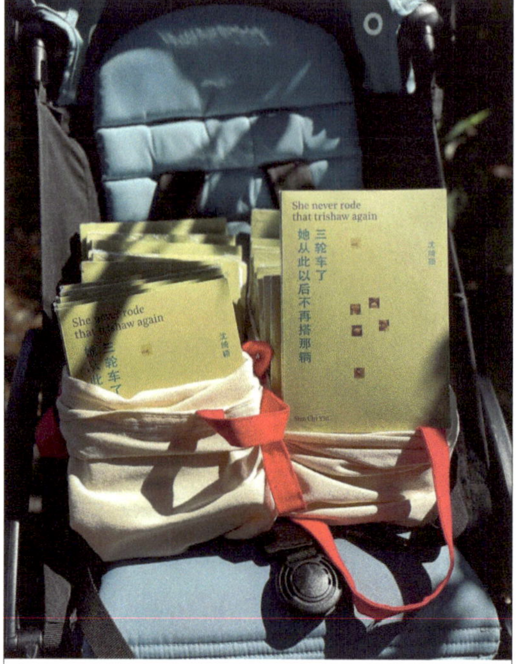

Liked by 396 others

chiyin_sim Borrowed Lucas Yiwei's stroller today to take another "baby" out!

First trip to the post office here in Berlin to ship 21 copies of my self-published and -distributed book "She Never Rode That Trishaw Again" to a buyer in Paris!

Thank you to all early buyers of the book from all over the world. We are beginning to work on shipping them from Berlin and Singapore.
(This book took longer than a 9 month gestation period! The broader project from which this is the first of what is likely to be three books, is going into its 9th year!!)

If you're keen on the book, please order here: http://chiyinsim.com/she-never-rode-that-trishaw-again/

For bulk orders please email studio@chiyinsim.com

If you'd like to use PayNow or bank transfer instead please just PM me. Thank you!

View all 8 comments

27 July 2021

world. What was already beneath his skin when he arrived? And I'm looking at the idea of *exposure*: When he was in utero, what was I already exposing him to, either consciously or subconsciously? My research has been about the anti-colonial war in British Malaya, so, throughout the pregnancy, I was digging around in war archives. I was looking at photographs of war and destruction and so-called 'acts of terrorism,' beheaded people and bodies. I began to contemplate what kind of exposure I had subjected him to before he even arrived and what it meant. I got to thinking about the skin as a means of exposure. You know, it's a layer that separates the inside from the outside, but it's also permeable.

In a nutshell, motherhood got me thinking about the possibilities of repair and restitution, the future, rather than being totally focused on past and trauma. It opened up, for me, a path that's more speculative and more about futurity – and that has been liberating.

"I was always a workaholic and now I'm forced to not work at the weekends because it's family time."

How has your *way* of making work changed, practically speaking?
Since my time is a lot more thinly sliced, I have to be a lot more efficient. I've definitely become less—well, I don't want to say "less reliable," given what I said before! I have learned to cut myself more slack in terms of being completely on the ball, all the time. I have to cut myself *a lot* more slack about those things. I've had to hire help sometimes—that means paying people to do the work that I can't. When I self-published a book last year, I had to hire help to distribute the book. I don't have the time now to literally stuff books into envelopes and get them out.

Also, it means working in a more collaborative manner. For instance, I've been invited to turn this family history project into a theatre performance. Many people said to me, "This is your material, you should be your own director!" and "You should write the script!" And

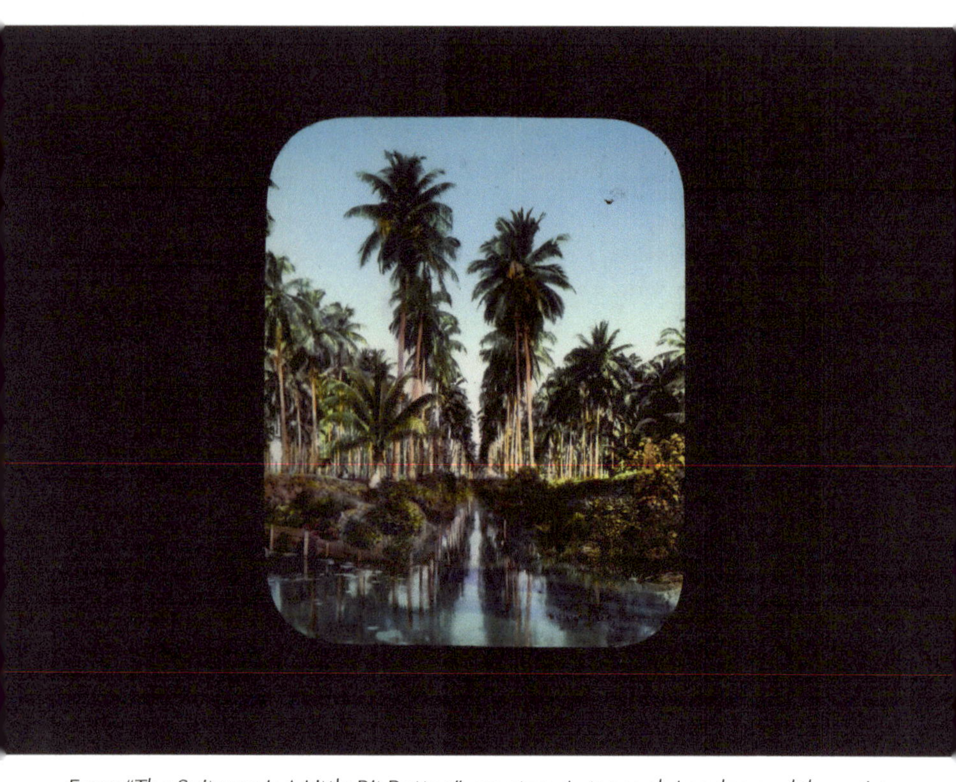

From "The Suitcase Is A Little Bit Rotten", courtesy Autograph London and the artist.

"I am going to be away a lot
in the coming year, which is something
that I feel bad and guilty about, but
it comes with the territory of
an art career getting off the ground."

I hear what they're saying, but with everything else I'm doing and with the way my life is set up right now, it's not possible. This is a full-scale theatrical production, so I've chosen to work in a much more collaborative way. I've brought in a director and a dramaturg. We're bringing on board a video artist, a stage designer, a production crew, and probably a sound artist, as well. So, that is a change, but is that a function of motherhood? Or is it the function of the fact that the work has gotten more complex and more multi-form?

It's definitely made me change the way I think about life. I mean, I was always a workaholic and now I'm forced to not work at the weekends because it's family time. I do have 'Mom Brain' much of the time. I'm definitely more absentminded. I have forgotten to defrost meat to make dinner many times. And, by the way, I'm also still trying to finish a PhD. So, it's definitely a big juggle. It's probably the hardest thing I've had to do in my life.

Did you have any notions about what it would be like to be an artist-mother before you had a kid?
No, I don't think I had any idea of how it was. I wasn't even close to people with young children. Mainly, I just took it as it came. I didn't think in great detail about what it would entail. Well, less travel, for sure, but I had gotten really tired of the constant travel being a photojournalist. Of course, the artist's life also comes with a lot of travel. I am going to be away a lot in the coming year, which is something that I feel bad and guilty about, but it comes with the territory of an art career getting off the ground. I've been asked to make an appearance at two art fairs and I have to do two two-week workshops for the theatrical production, so it's all a part of making new work and getting the work to new audiences. I've had a couple of substantial museum acquisitions and so it's good to go and connect personally. Lining up help while I'm away is also difficult and extremely expensive in New York, so it's definitely a real struggle. In New York, the financial question looms very, very large.

There's a lot of guilt and judgment heaped on moms for traveling too much. Have you brushed up against that at all?
Definitely. And that doesn't happen with the dads for sure. I did my first trip away from Lucas in Arles 2021 when I had a solo show. Oftentimes I'll now ask myself, "Do I *really* have to go?" But with a solo show, of course you have to go. I always question myself about it but, you know, every time the boys have a good time. Mom's away! They can eat ketchup and ice cream all they want!

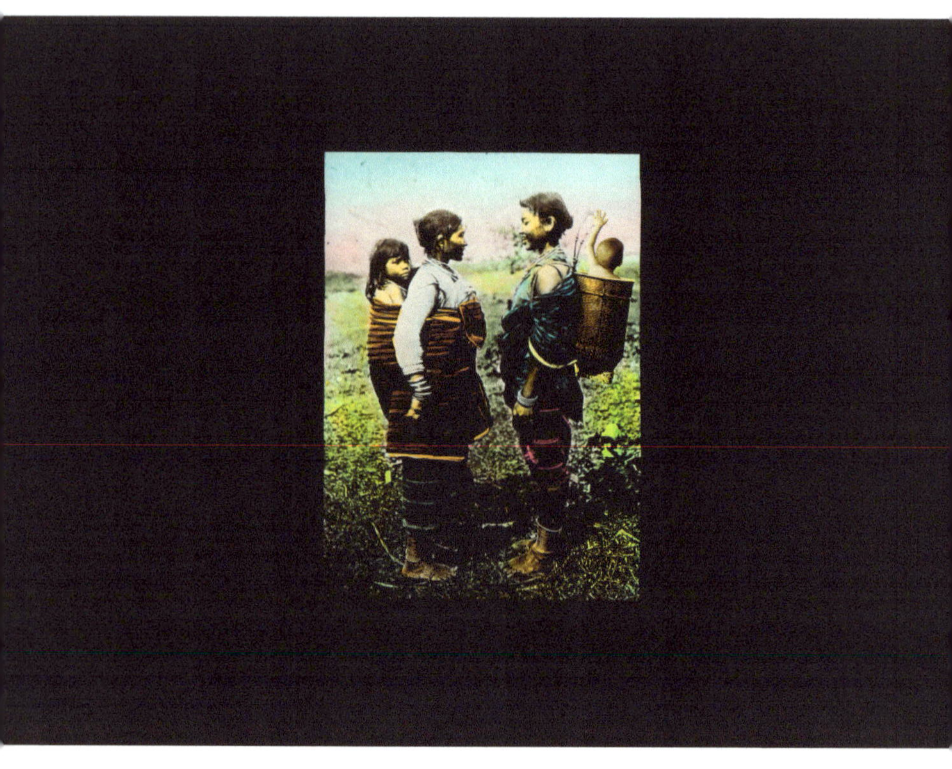

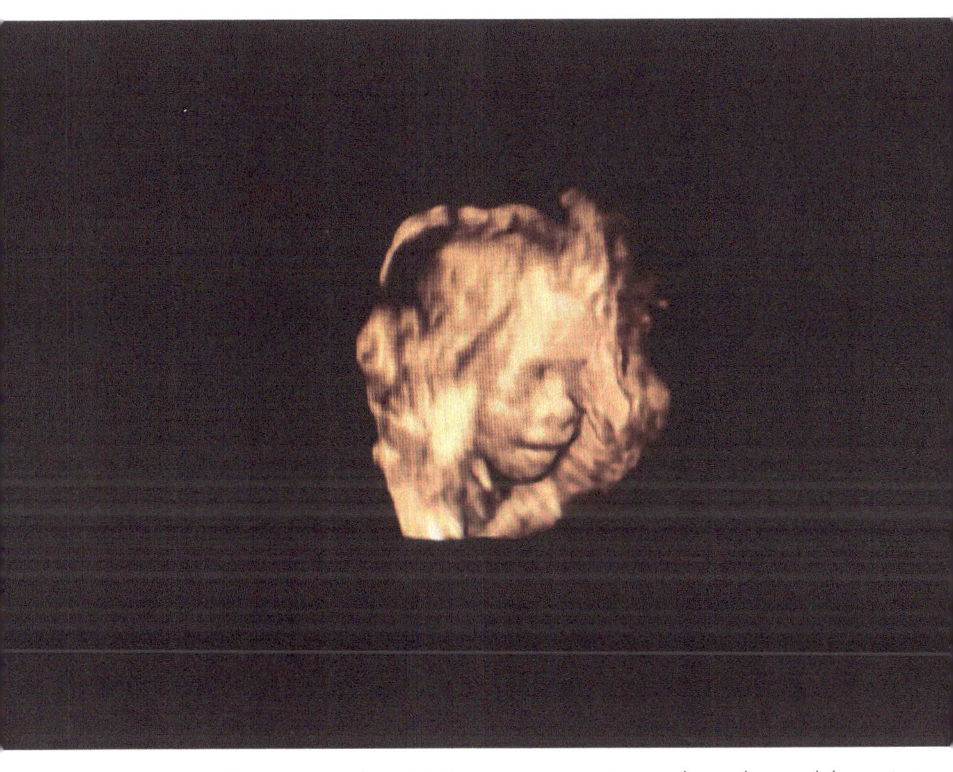

From "The Suitcase Is A Little Bit Rotten", courtesy Autograph London and the artist.

You mentioned that you've moved base three times in the last two years. How has that been with a small child?
Very difficult, though I've come to conclude that it's not really about the small child, it's more about the relocation itself. Adults need to adjust, too. It took us months to adjust and every time there are all these practical matters to solve: We always have to look for a new house, look for a new preschool, look for new nannies. Then set up the house, and make it childproof, and so on.

He was born in London, and then at six months old, we took him to Singapore and we were there for eight months before moving to Berlin. With each move, he sometimes seems happy on the surface, but then there's always signs that he is adjusting. When we moved from Singapore to Berlin, Lucas didn't eat solids for the first three weeks we were there. No matter what I cooked, no matter how I tried to replicate exactly what he ate in Singapore, he just refused all foods and would only drink milk. Then when we moved from Berlin to New York, we really talked it up to him, and he got excited, but then sleep was a problem. He wouldn't sleep without me holding his hand for many weeks in those initial months, but now we just have to say goodnight and close the door. I know people like to say it's fine to move young kids around before they are school-aged, because they're not tied down by the school schedule yet, but we don't find it to be that true. *Every time* it's been an adjustment.

So, relocating with a young child adds pragmatic difficulties, but I think it's hard enough for adults. I'm not sure that *I'm* fully settled here, you know?

In one of the "Letters to Lucas" series that you've been publishing, you write of your experience as a "geriatric" mother. How do you think being in your forties as a first-time mom has affected the experience?
There's pluses and minuses. The pluses are that I'm on my third career, so I've done a lot of shit in my life already. I already know what I'm about, so I'm not still trying to 'figure myself out' and that kind of stuff. I sometimes talk about being #toooldtogiveashit. I'm more irreverent at this stage in life. There's a lot of stuff that I don't have time for, and I call bullshit bullshit. You can say I'm set in my ways, but really, I know what I'm about.

The minuses are many as well. Physical ones are probably the most prominent among them. I just don't have the same energy that I had

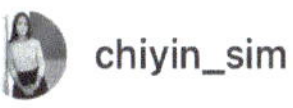

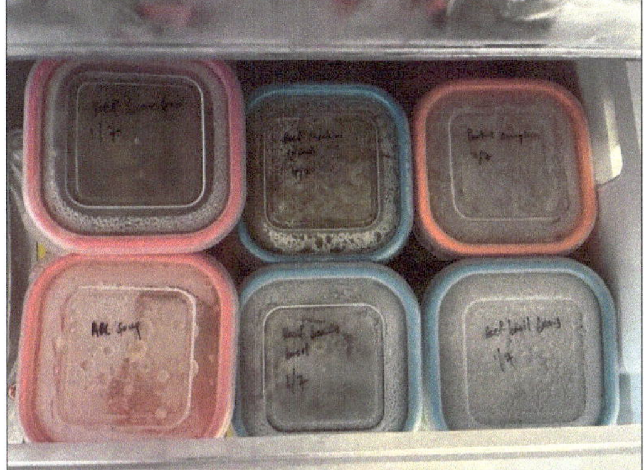

Liked by **161 others**

chiyin_sim Fellow #artistmums #artistparents, advice please: do you write into grant applications the cost of childcare in lieu of your absence — when you have to go away on installation trips, weeks-long workshops, to biennale openings etc and can't take your child, or have to bring them and need the help where you are so you can work?

As supportive as one's spouse/partner can be, they too have their own full-time jobs and careers. And we do not all have the blessing of extended family close by or able to help.

How do you all do it? How does one factor in these additional costs? Have you ever successfully gotten childcare costs covered as an item in an arts grant?

Separation already comes laden with other forms of sacrifice, cost and anxieties for all working mothers / parents, but are there ways we can get help at least with the financial cost? It's a real conundrum to this still-newish mum.. as international art/work travel picks up again. Thanks in advance! @nomaternityleave @ani.liu.studio @helenahaimes #artmamas

View all 6 comments

12 August 2022

"Who is supposed to pay for the labor that is needed to look after the kids while we work?"

when I was 25 or even 35. I'm 45 this year, and I don't have the physical strength that I once had. I mean, the 21-year-old me backpacked around China with a heavy backpack and could do the squat toilets with no problem. When I was a documentary photographer and filmmaker, I carried all that crap myself. But now, even this 12-kilogram kid is about to give me a hernia. Now, I'm in the worst shape that I've ever been because motherhood has dovetailed with middle age and that's really a recipe for disaster. I used to be quite fit but, as a mom, I haven't been able to make time to exercise much. I really want and need to make time for that.

How have you made being an artist-mother work for you?
I think I'm just trying to make it work. I don't know which other way there is, and part of the time it's *not* working. I mean, I feel like I'm constantly drowning. So, I can't really say that it is working, but I'm getting new commissions, new shows and fellowships. I'm making new books and performances. So, the work is carrying on. It's progressing, even if slowly. The most important thing is that I feel I'm learning, growing and trying new things, evolving in my work and life.

I think most of the time it *doesn't* work. Who is supposed to pay for the labor that is needed to look after the kids while we work? I don't know if there are many arts bodies that would pay for childcare. Grantmakers and institutions don't really have a provision for people who have children. Family-friendly residencies are extremely few and far between. When I did a residency after Lucas was born, they express sympathies and understanding, but I had to pay for an apartment because the provision was for a single person to share a flat. So, I had to spend my own money in order to make the residency happen—otherwise it would mean giving up on the opportunity to do the residency, which was a very fruitful and important one in my career. You can accept it's just the cost of doing business and pay the extra expenses to house your partner and child and maybe for a bit of childcare, but you know, it would be helpful if grantmakers allowed artist-parents to file childcare costs as part of the expense because it *is* the cost of doing business. If I have to go away to install and open a show at a biennial for a whole week, there's *a cost* that comes with that because that means I'm not around to provide the childcare. Even if he goes to school, there's the after-school care, there's the dinner making, and you can't calculate for your partner to be available every single day, all the time, to pick up that slack. Parenting is a two-person job for the most part. And so it would be extremely helpful if institutions took that cost into consideration. I think the more people are open about the fact that they have young children – and I say this of both mothers and fathers – the more apparent it will be that this is a real need that they have to support.

I do feel like this conversation is not happening really amongst fathers somehow, that the fathers don't need to apologize for having children. But I'm applying for a grant now and will add the childcare expenses just to see what happens. I'm going to experiment with being radically open. Maybe it's going to hurt me – maybe it has already hurt me in ways I don't know – but life is an experiment.

chiyinsim.com

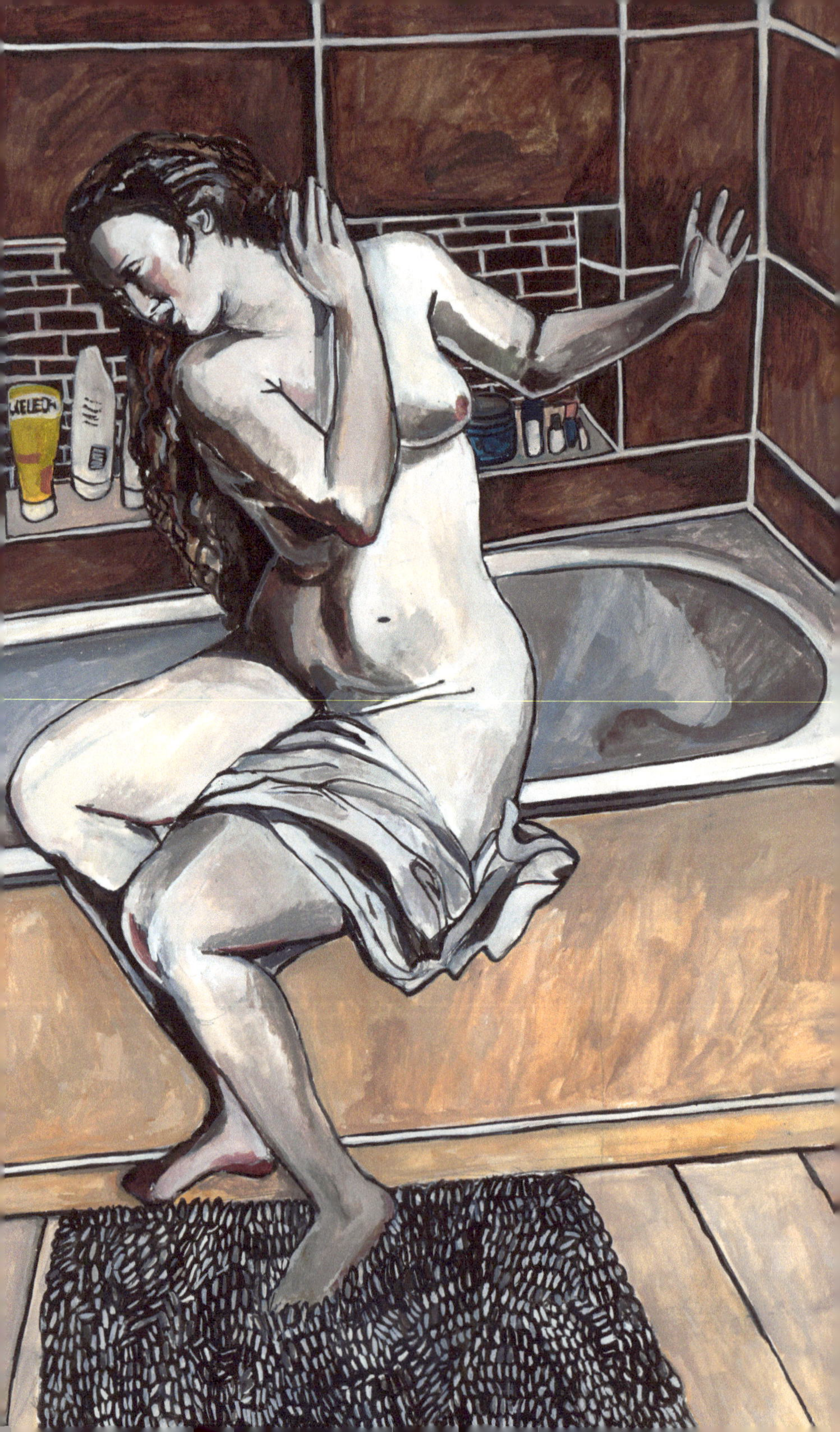

Sarah **Lightman**
b. 1975 UK

Biblical Domestic
2021-22

Women from the bible are thrust into modern domestic trials in this tongue-in-cheek series of watercolors by Sarah Lightman. At first blush, the paintings offer a joke of simple anachronism. Yet, the dark comedy emerges as a fast aftertaste: the women have escaped their roles in the master paintings of yore only to become trapped in household chores.

Life during lockdown only served to exacerbate gender inequality. While many people were forced to work from home, housework and childcare, two of the great obstacles to ambition, did not get distributed equally.

Lightman's work has long held as a goal the restoration of female agency in artworks. In 2019, she completed her PhD thesis, "Dressing Eve and Other Reparative Acts in Women's Comics." With a special interest in graphic narratives and comics, she emphasizes the importance of bringing women's issues into the work: "If women knew, and talked more, about the things that they did and the things that happened to them and things their bodies went through, what a different experience we'd all have of our lives."

sarahlightman.com

Opposite:
Just Ten Minutes Peace (2022)
Watercolor on paper, 297 x 420 mm

Susanna begs her family for ten minutes, just ten minutes,
of uninterrupted solitude, so she can have her bath in peace.

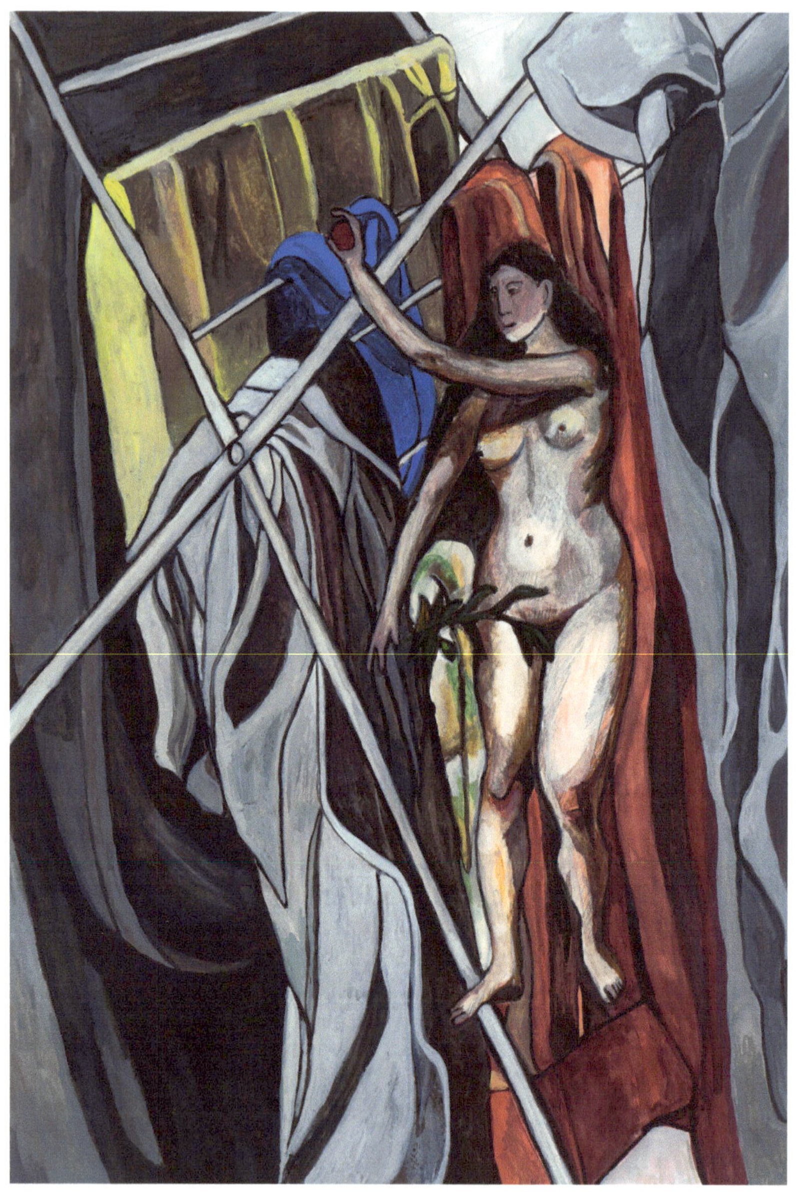

Dressing Eve During a Pandemic (2021)
Watercolor on paper, 297 x 420 mm

Here is Eve from a painting by Titian entitled "The Fall of Man" (1550),
during my own fall as mother/artist/homeschooler.

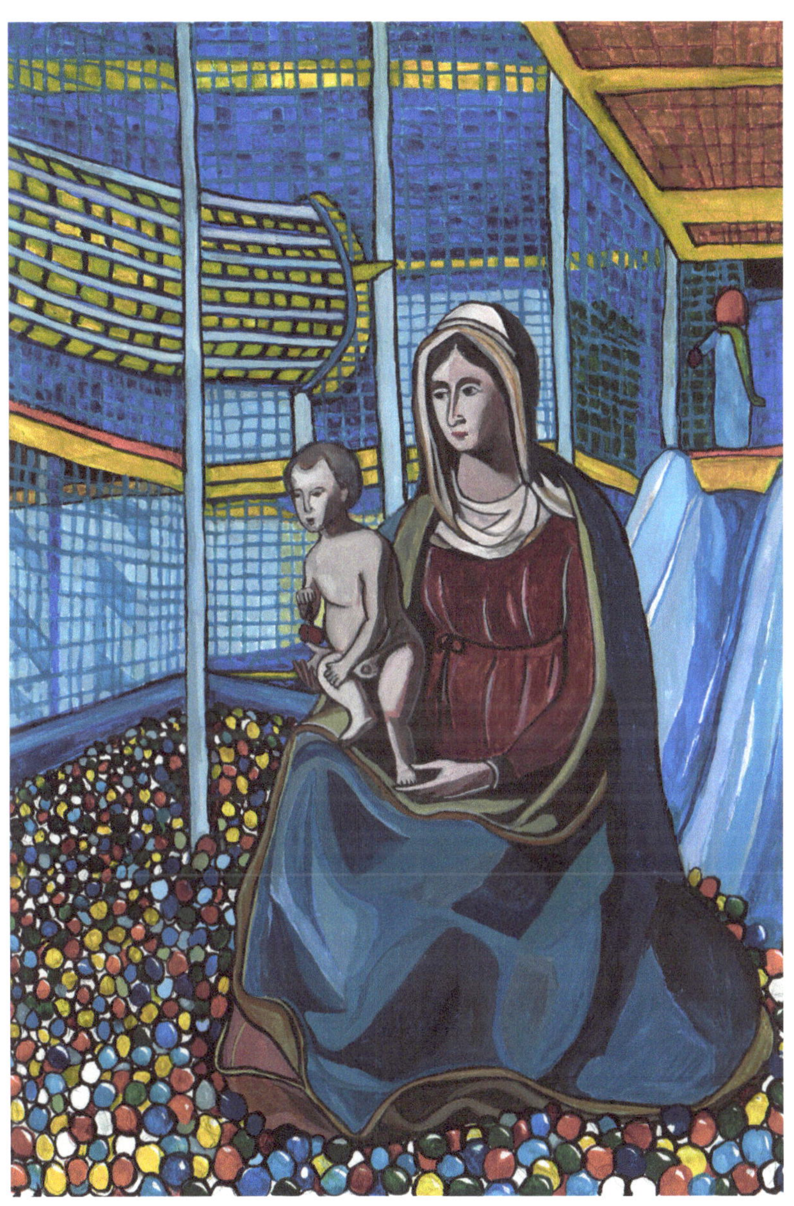

Madonna of the Soft Play - A Prayer for the Lost and Found (2022)
Watercolor on paper, 297 x 420 mm

Mary wonders if she needs to dig deep into the ball pit for Jesus's missing nappy, or should she leave it as a surprise lucky dip for the next visitor? More pressingly, where did he pick up those cherries he was enjoying so much, and are they even edible?

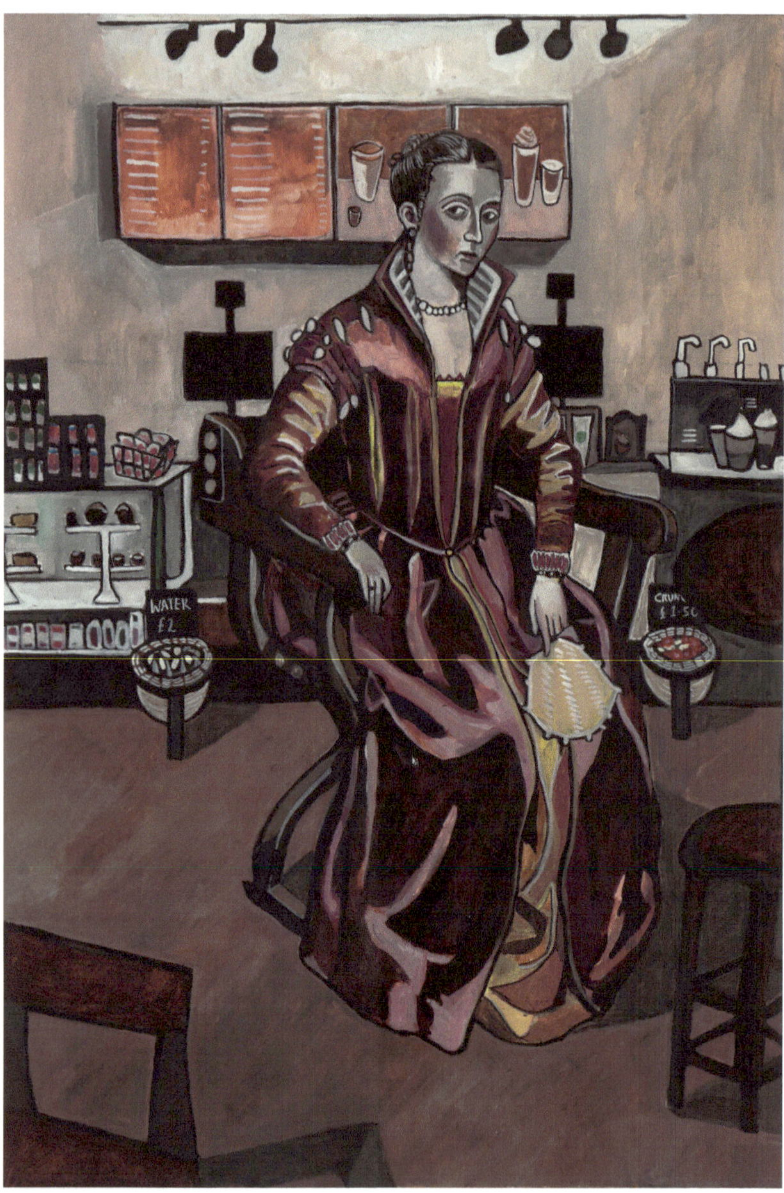

Novice School Rep. for Year 3 (2022)
Watercolor on paper, 297 x 420 mm

This Lady in Red had been so excited about being chosen to be a School Rep. that she arrived two hours early for the meeting at Starbucks, on St. John's Wood High Street. She was, perhaps, just a little over-dressed for the occasion but she had always found it tricky to calibrate the very best way to make exactly the right impression to the other mums at the school.

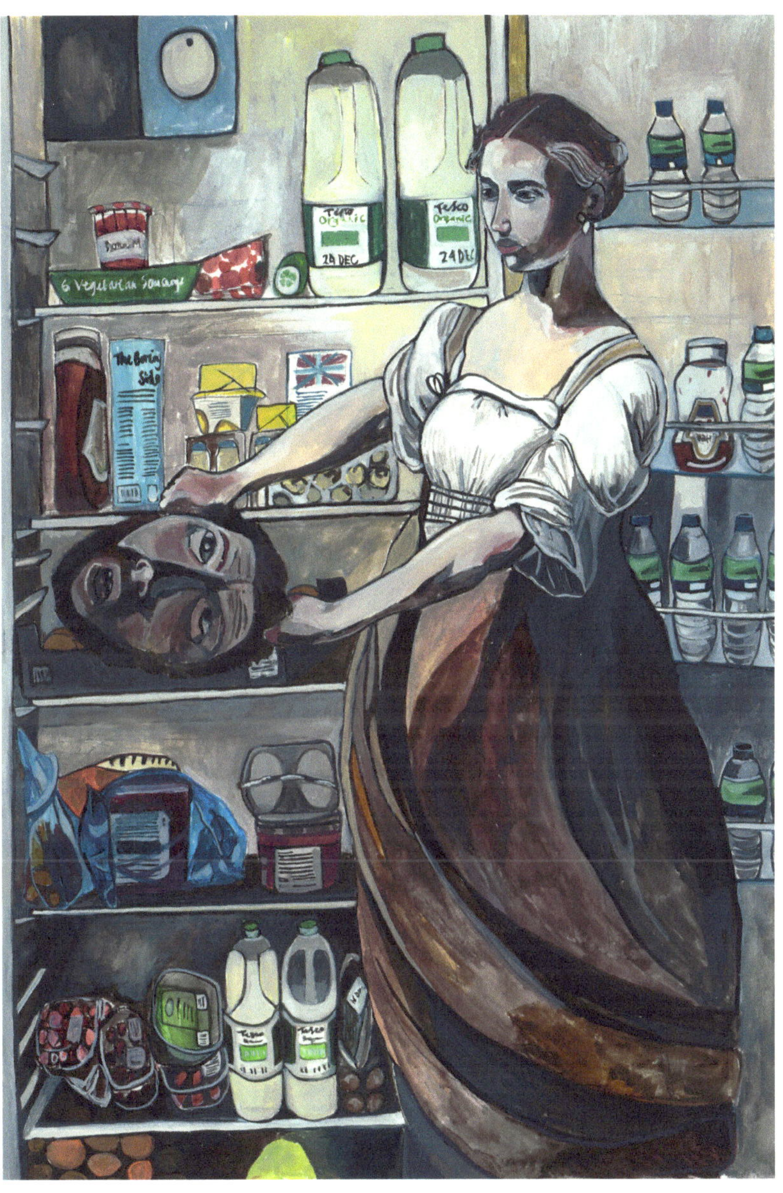

Fridge Frustrations (2022)
Watercolor on paper, 297 x 420 mm

Judith can't find anywhere in the fridge for her organic and fresh cut of Holofernes. Once again, her eyes were bigger than her storage space. When will she learn not to lose her head over all those delicious special offers?

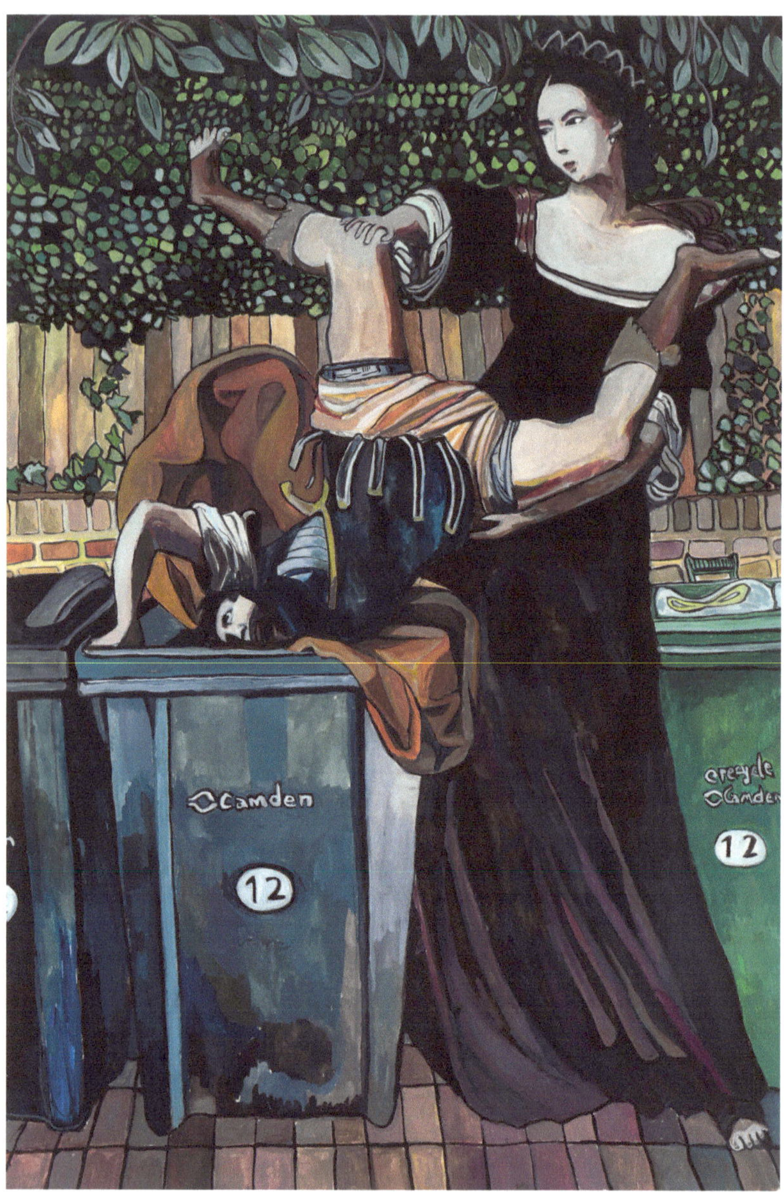

Refuse (2022)
Watercolor on paper, 297 x 420 mm

In the Borough of Camden, the refuse men come on alternate
Tuesday mornings for the black bins. Timoclea finds it a
struggle to fit in all her rubbish on a Monday night. She often
has to give everything a big shove.

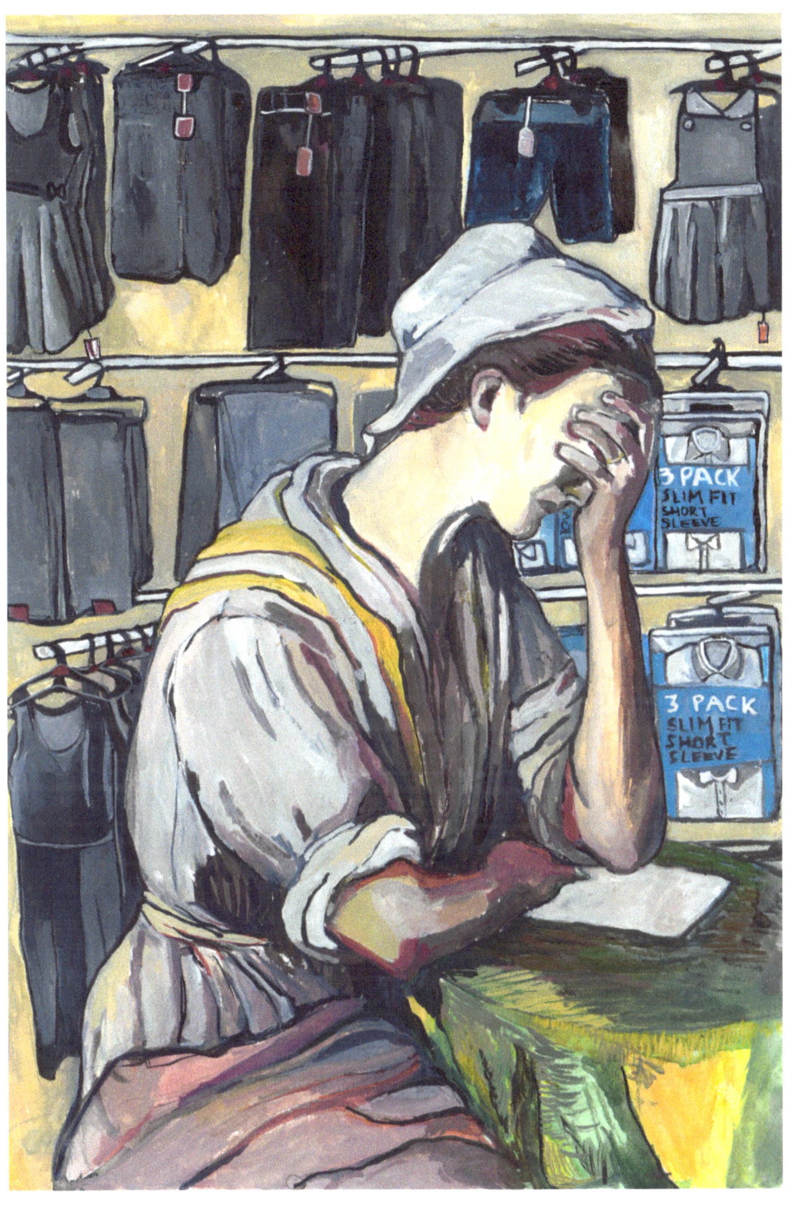

The Uniform List Blues and Greys (2022)
Watercolor on paper, 297 x 420 mm

As September approaches she is struck by a deep overwhelming malaise as she opens the dreaded email from the school secretary with the full list of uniform requirements for the upcoming academic year. And then, before she knows it, term is about to start, and she realizes that everywhere is sold out of knee high socks in the right size.

Sarah Lightman

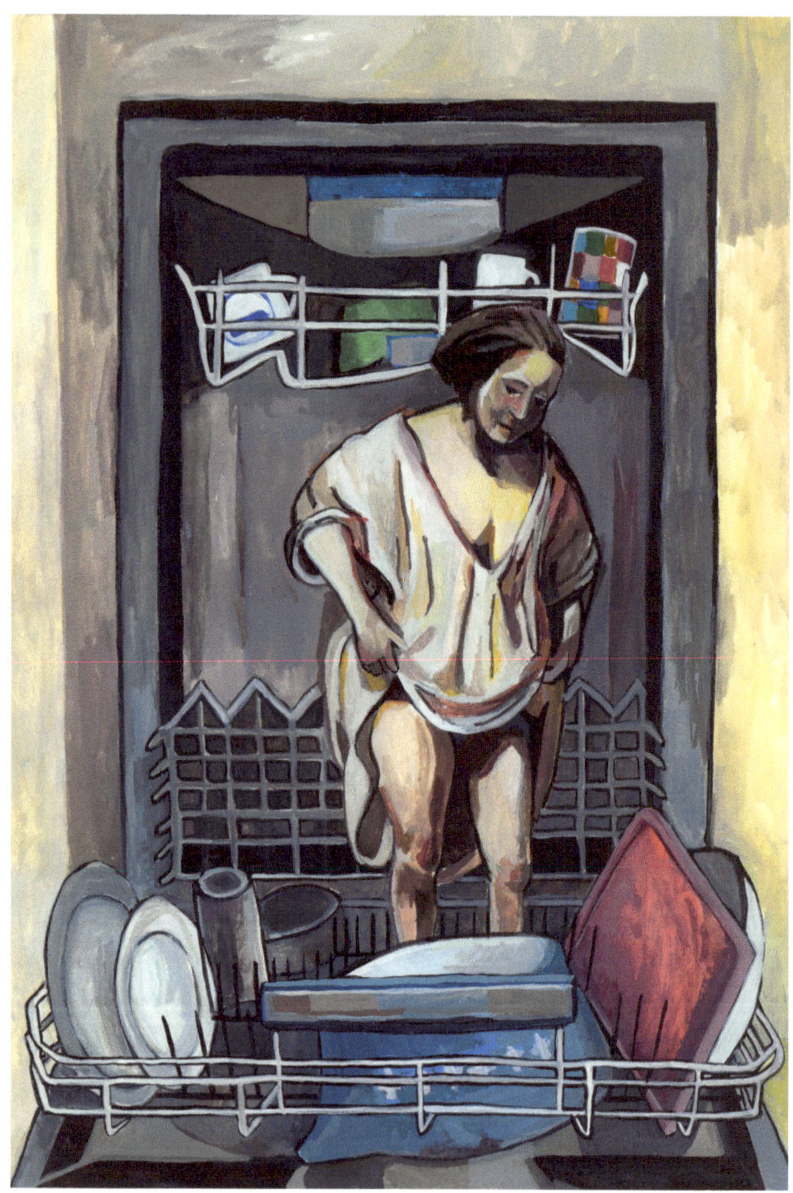

Woman Wading in a Stream of Stir Fry {Bathsheba} (2021)
Watercolor on paper, 297 x 420 mm

No sooner does she escape Rembrandt's murky waters, Bathsheba
finds herself stuck in puddles of last night's stir fry as someone,
once again, forgot to switch on the dishwasher.

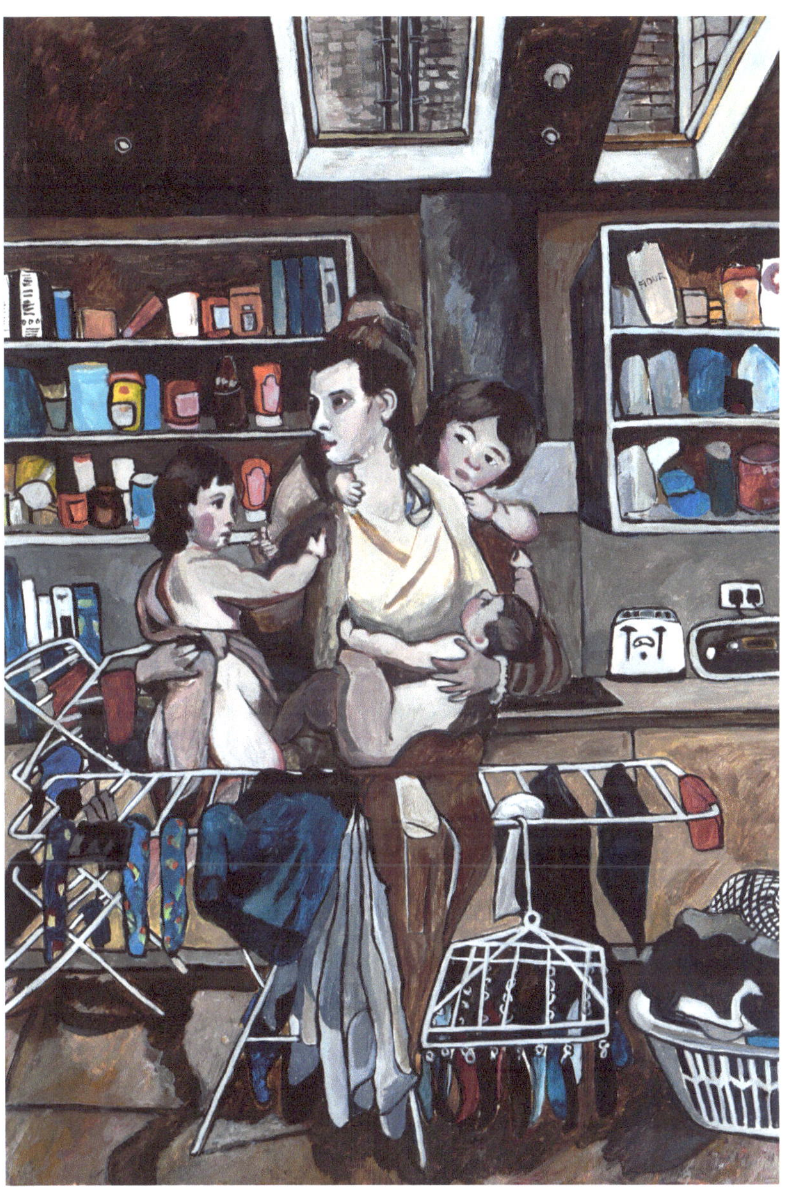

Lady Cockburn, and her Three Sons, Count the Seconds until Their Cleaner and Nanny Arrive (2022)
Watercolor on paper, 297 x 420 mm

She is beyond words at this point.

Sarah Lightman

C.S. Griffel
b. 1972 USA

A Mother's Solitude

My bank balance is negative.
Bills stack up;
I tuck them in nooks
to avoid remembering
that I can't pay.

Half my furniture wobbles—Broken,
like my marriage that ended.
Hell, *because* of my marriage that ended.
The kitchen table and chairs
only hold together with glue and
sheer will.

But sometimes,
I wake up and sit at my
failing kitchen table,
sipping a hot cup of tea and looking
out the window as the sun slowly rises,
casting a pink hue on wispy clouds.

A solitude descends
that only mothers know:
a peacefully sleeping child,
the joy of silence,
and a dawning realization
that I am not miserable.

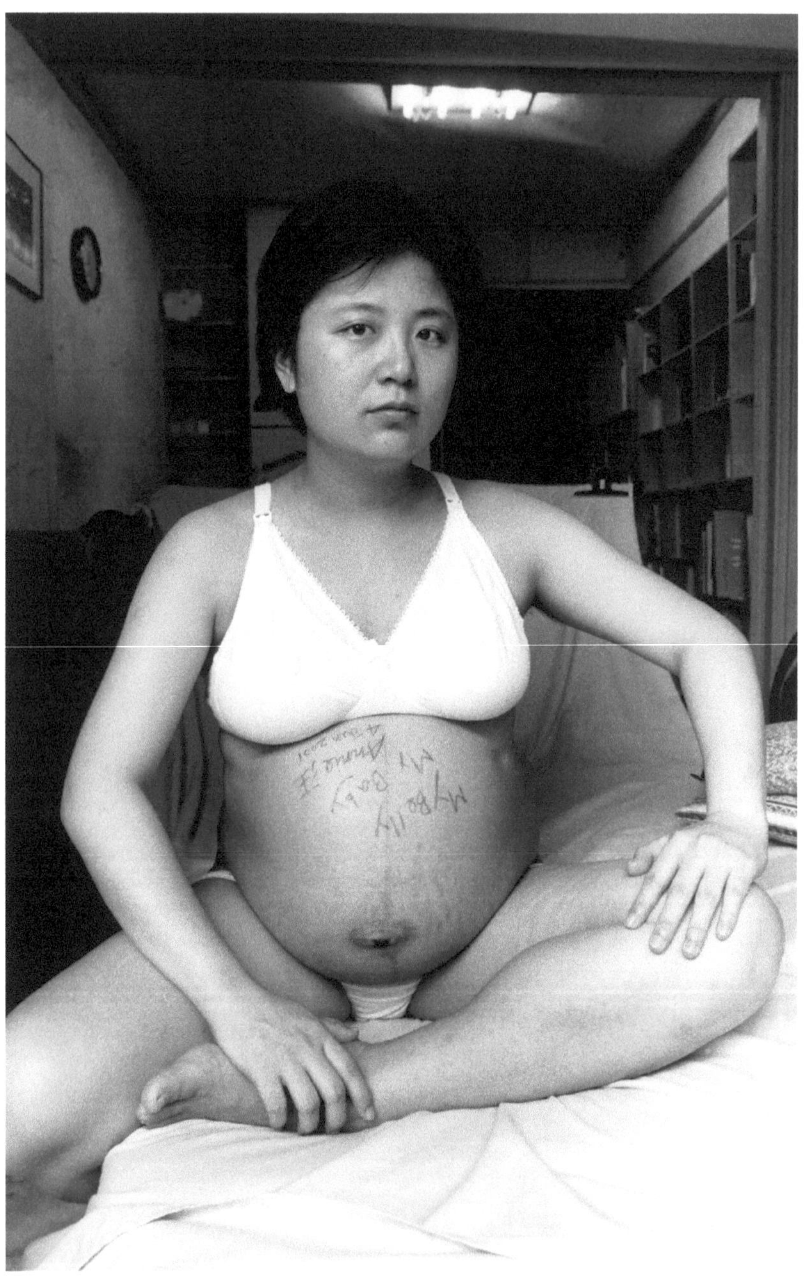

The Mother as a Creator No.1: The day before I was due to give birth (2001).

Annie Hsiao-Ching **Wang**
b. 1972 Taiwan

The Mother as a Creator
2001 - ongoing

Wang's photobiographical series is more than two decades in the making: She began the project in 2001 before giving birth, with each new photo featuring a print of the previous image, marking the passage of time alongside major milestones, such as the moment when her son reaches the same height as her.

She writes of her motivation: "Motherhood is a long-term process full of a myriad of complex feelings. This complexity cannot be expressed solely by saccharine images of Mother and Child, nor by the image of the Mother Incarnate willingly sacrificing herself for the sake of her children. All of these stereotypes of Motherhood are for me a tedious, unavoidable harangue which offers me no consolation."

Her black and white images are pensive and sometimes playful, careful in their composition by contrast to the fast-moving snapshots of daily life. Wang offers a profound vision of the ongoing course of motherhood.

artanniewang.weebly.com

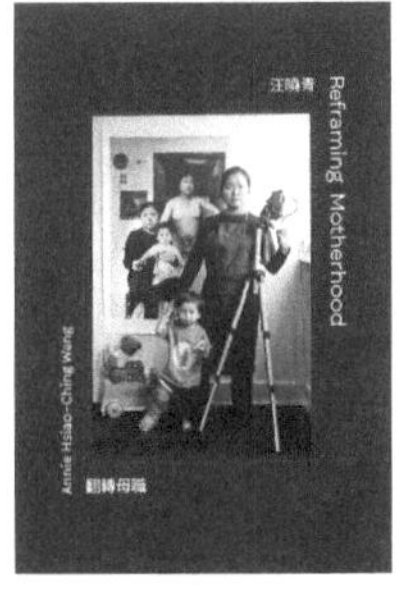

Reframing Motherhood
Hardback
78 pages
Chinese / English / Korean
BO Books, Sept. 2020
ISBN 9791197119101
€37

moom.cat

Annie Hsiao-Ching Wang

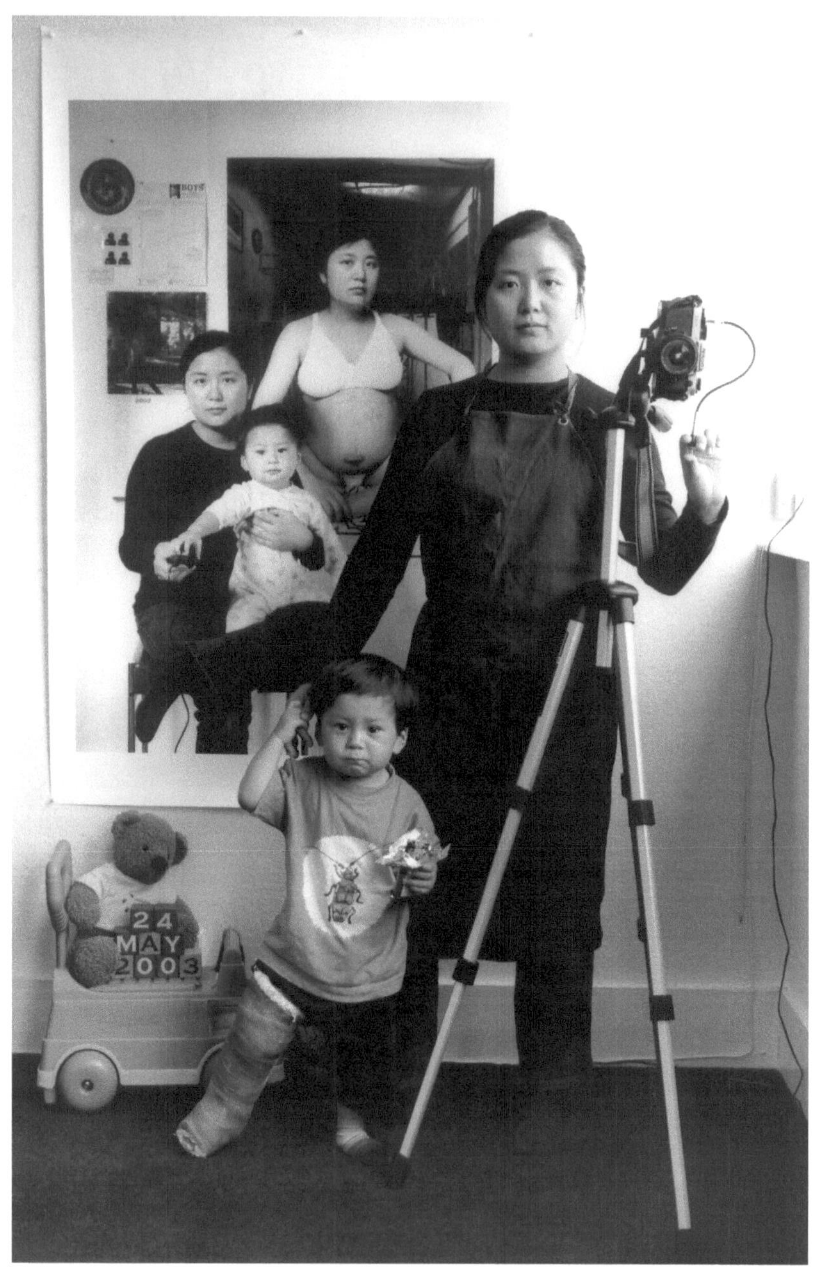

The Mother as a Creator No. 3: My son's leg in a cast (2003).

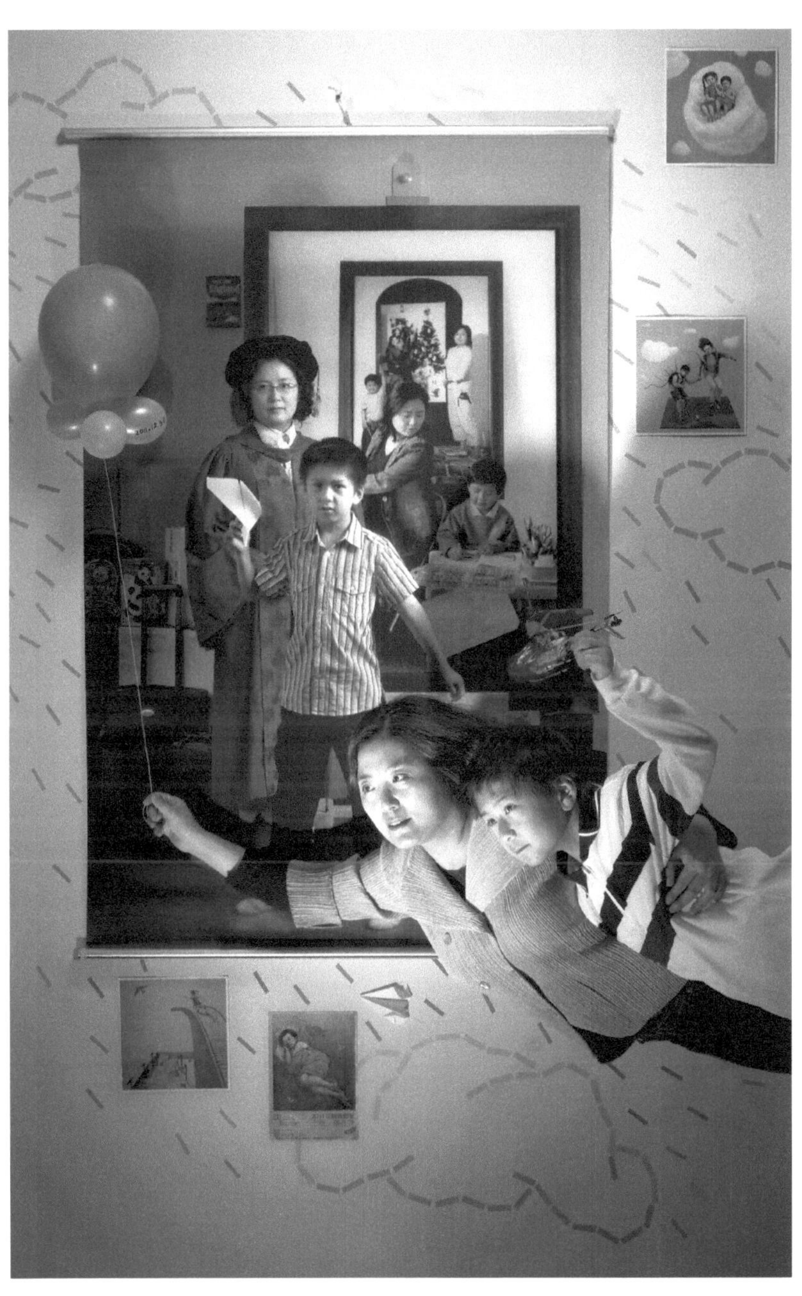

The Mother as a Creator No. 8: Making dreams (2011).

Annie Hsiao-Ching Wang

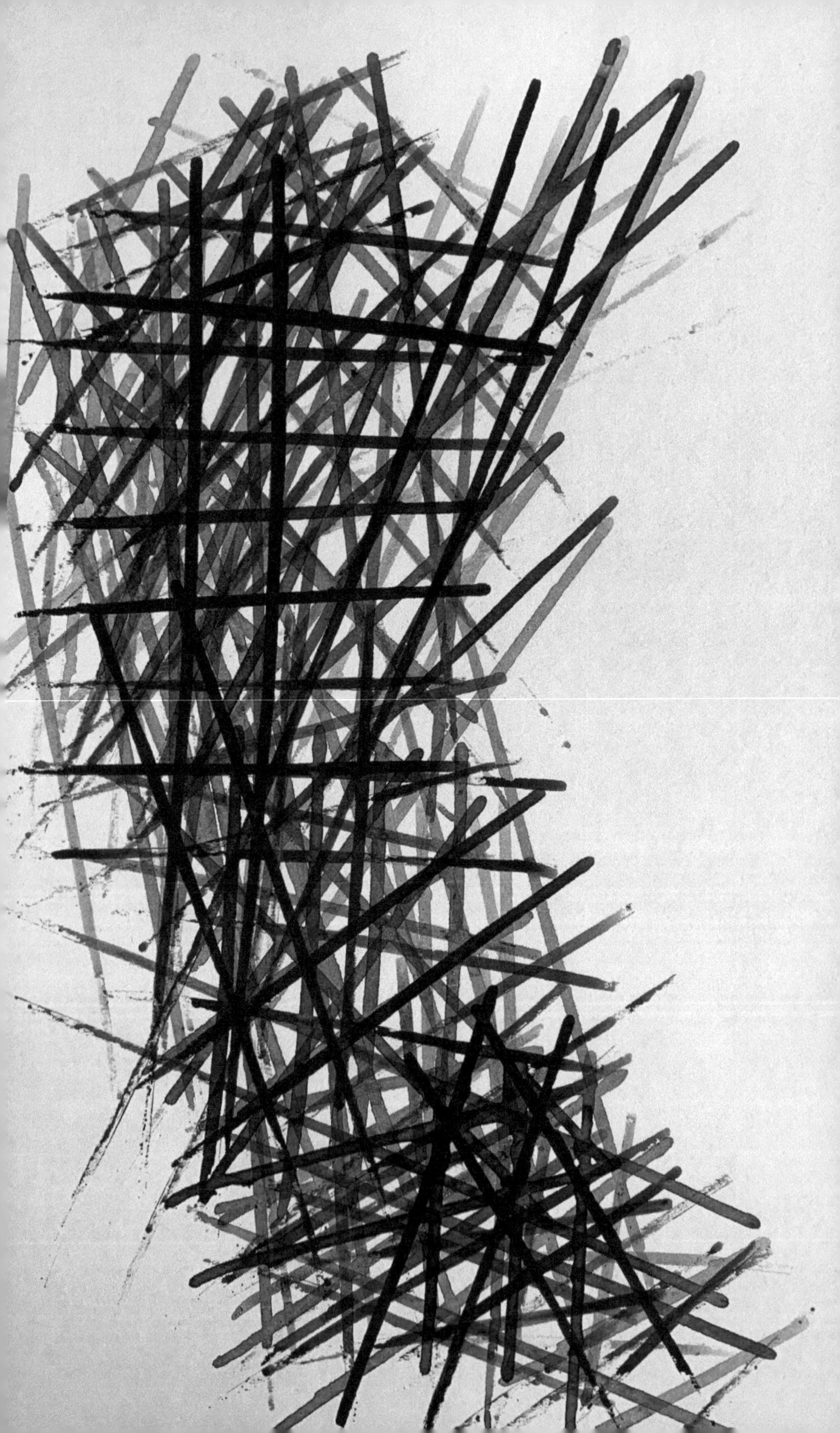

Rachael **Grad**
b. 1976 Canada

Motherhood Hit Me Like a Train
2021-22

"When I became a mother, my art changed course," says Rachael Grad. "Toys overtook my home and artwork."

Grad created this series of paintings using one of the new residents of her home: Thomas the Tank Engine. She dips the trains in ink or watercolor and then drives it over paper, again and again. The geometrical precision of the straight train tracks suggests something orderly, but the resulting patterns are busy and dizzying, anxious in their methodical repetition. The sameness of the sweeping marks, which Grad describes as "unexpectedly tiring for my arm and back," is familiar to parents of small children, who find themselves performing the same duties, singing the same songs, and playing with the same toys in the ritualistic fervor of a litany.

rachaelgrad.com

Opposite:
Grey Line #9 (2022)
Ink on Paper, 9 x 12 inches

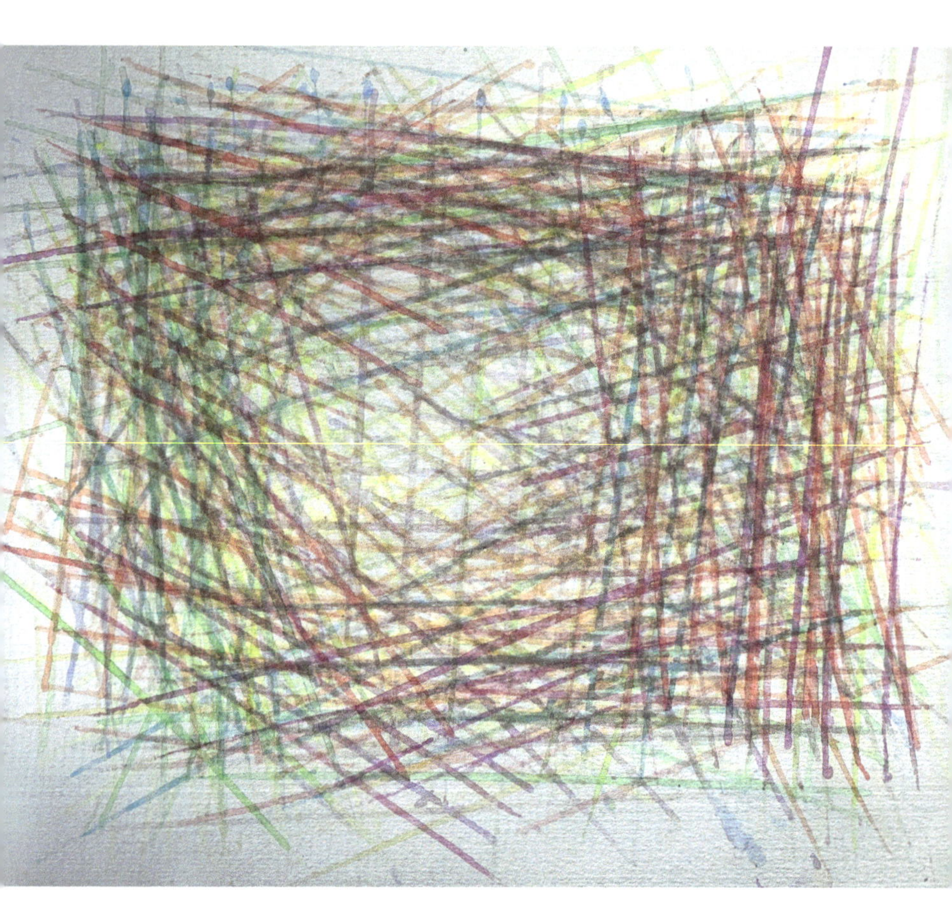

Route #2 (2021)
Watercolor on paper, 14 x 11 inches

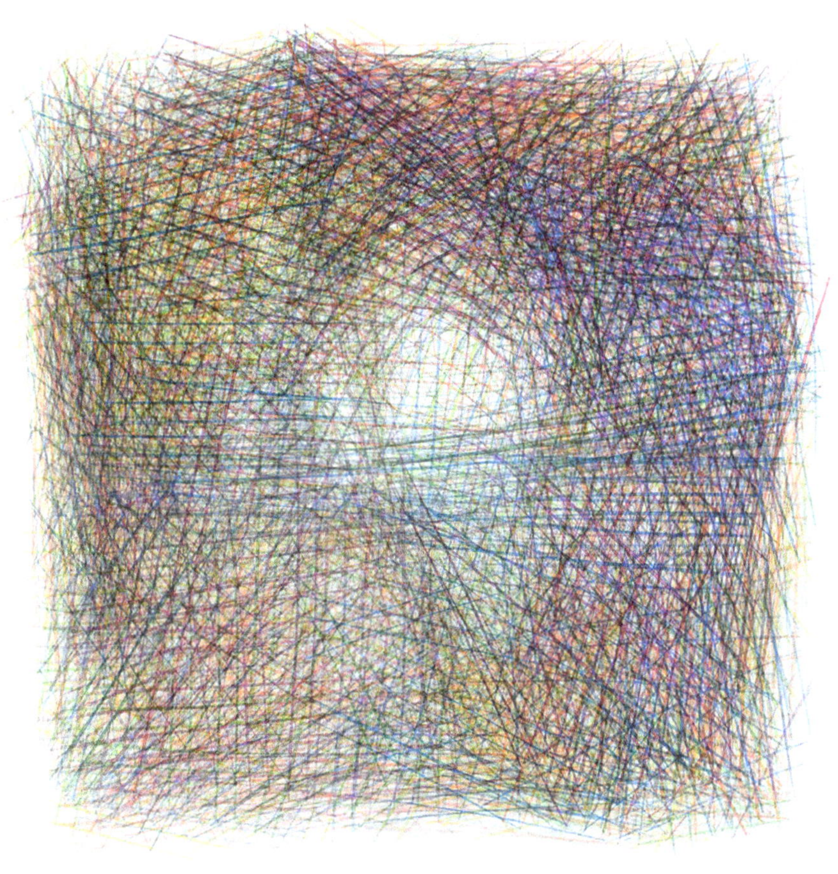

Cross-Country #2 (2021-22)
Watercolor on paper, 36 x 36 inches

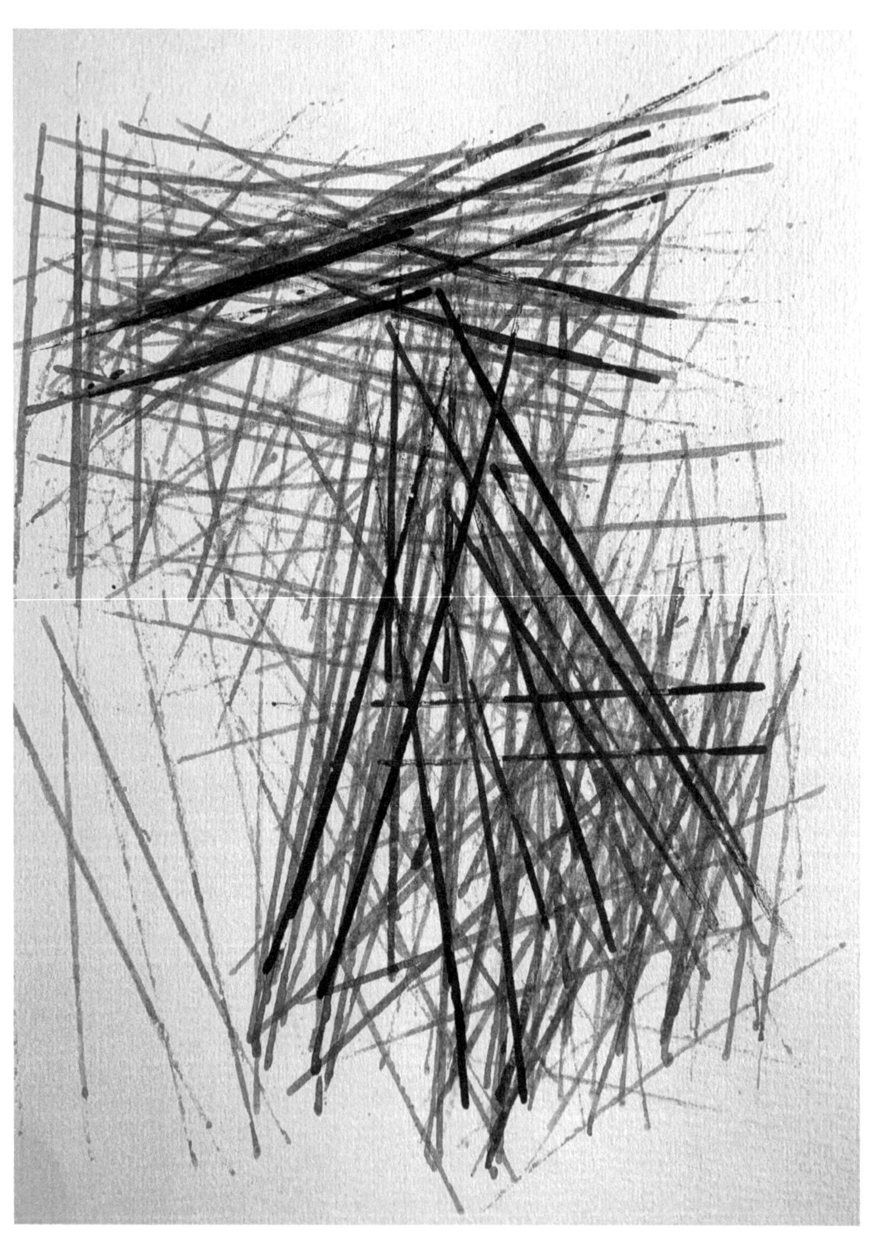

Grey Line #4 (2021)
Ink on paper, 11 x 14 inches

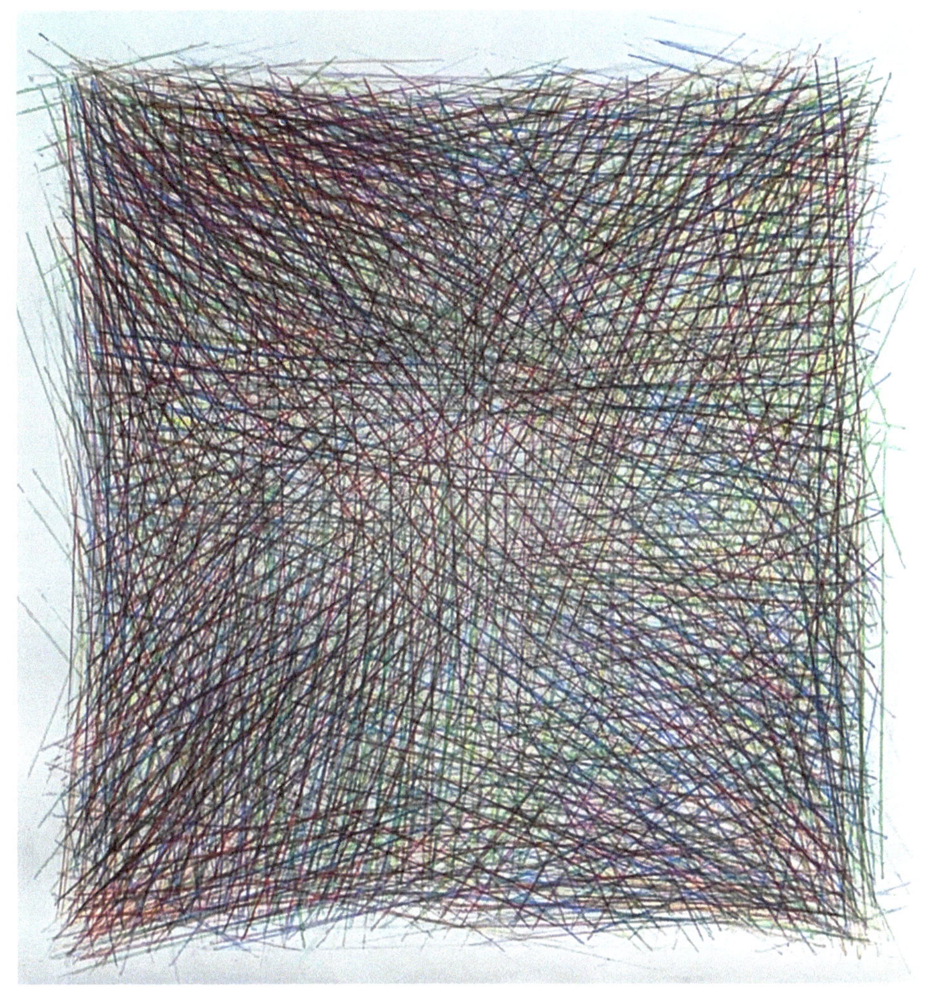

Cross-Country #3 (2021-22)
Watercolor on paper, 36 x 36 inches

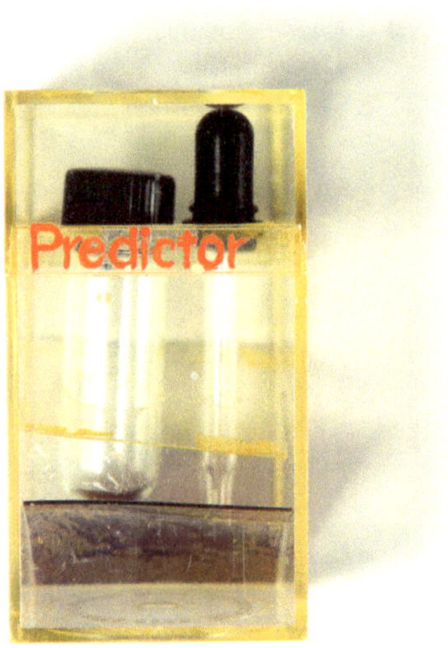

Predictor Home Pregnancy Test Kit, 1971, designed by Meg Crane.
Image courtesy Brendan McCabe

Designing Motherhood

Things That Make and Break Our Births

by Michelle Millar Fisher and Amber Winick

Who designs the experience of motherhood, and how? What products are available, how are they advertised and used, and who really benefits from them? Often, because of the shame cast upon periods, sex, and pregnancy, much is left unknown and undiscussed. The authors write in the introduction: "In this book we cast a critical eye on the designs that govern the choice (or lack of choice) to give birth, that mold motherhood across intersections, that ensure that people can remain childfree, and that ultimately shape every living person."

Designing Motherhood offers insight into the at-home pregnancy test, tools for cervical exams, period tracking apps, tampons and period cups, panty shields for staying "fresh," and birth control devices like the IUD. The book asks that we consider too how the experiences of sex, pregnancy, and birth are portrayed in photography and film.

Part-documentation and part-polemic, *Designing Motherhood* ventures beyond product descriptions into the messy fights along the way. This makes transparent the battleground nature of the body, and emphasizes how designs become inherently political.

designingmotherhood.org

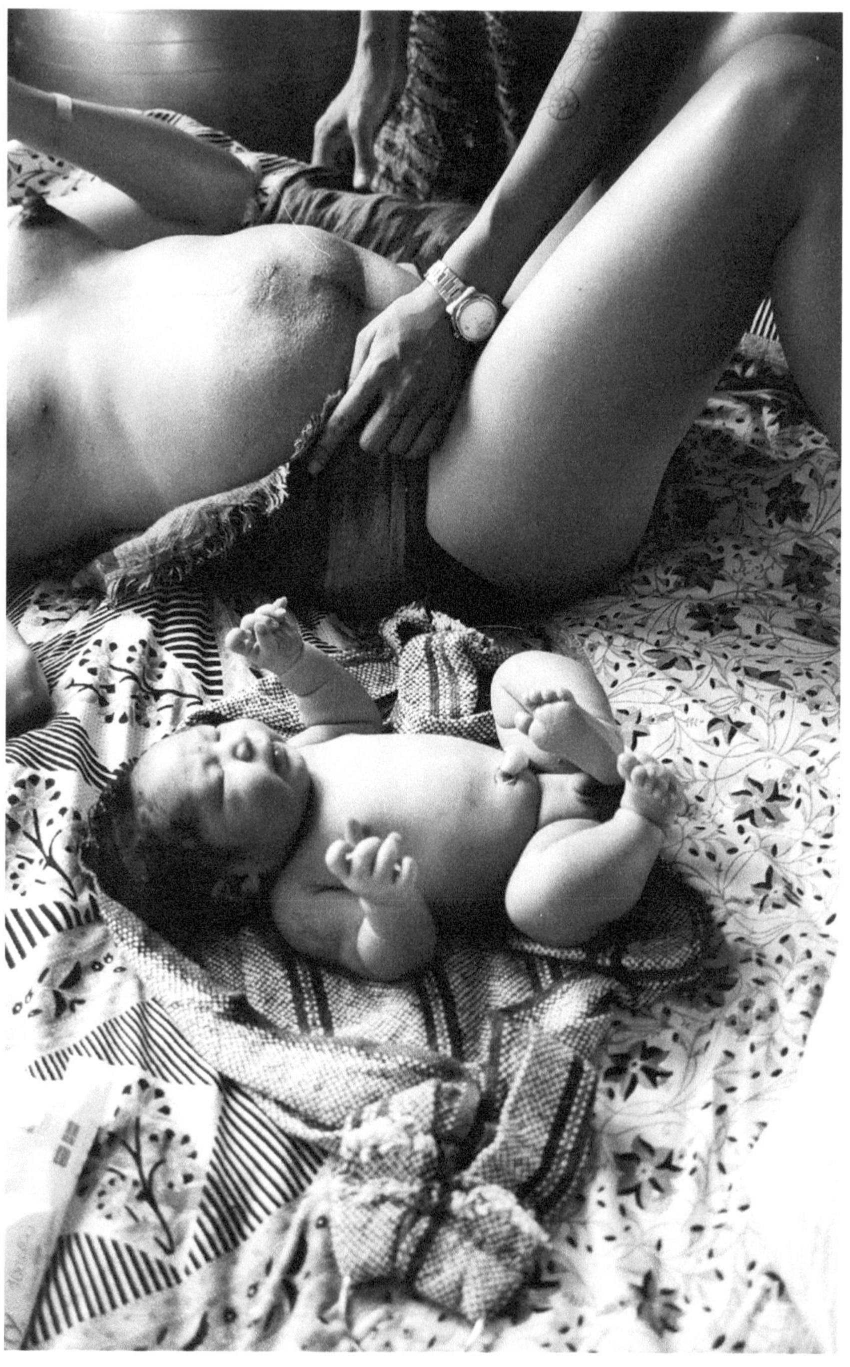

Postpartum faja wrap, California.
Image courtesy of Sophia Harris

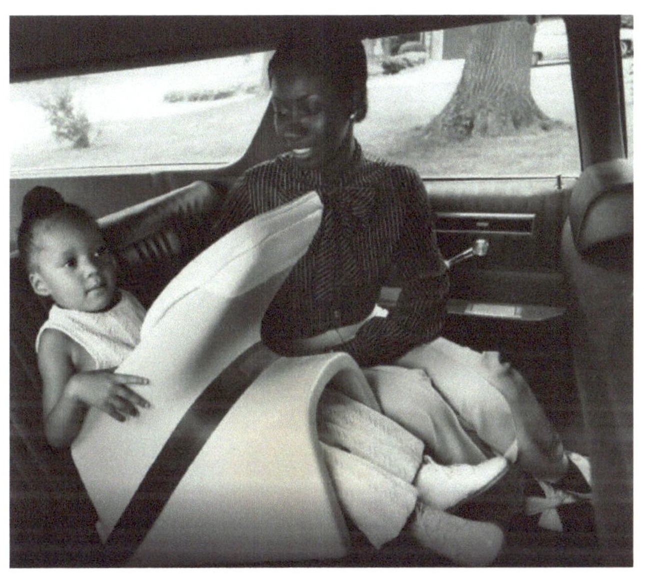

Ford Motor Company's "Tot-Guard" 1973.
Image courtesy of the Collections of The Henry Ford Museum

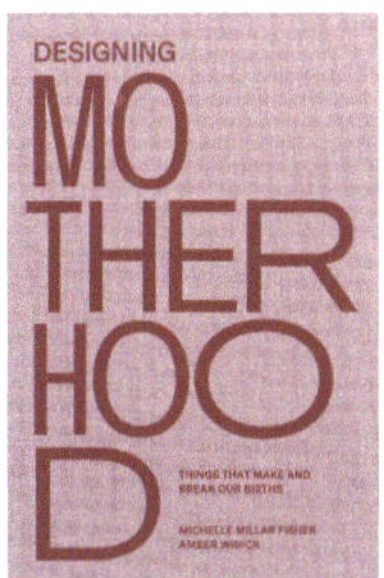

Hardback
344 pages
7 x 10" / 17.8 x 25.4 cm
MIT Press, Sept. 2021
ISBN 9780262044899
$44.95

mitpress.mit.edu

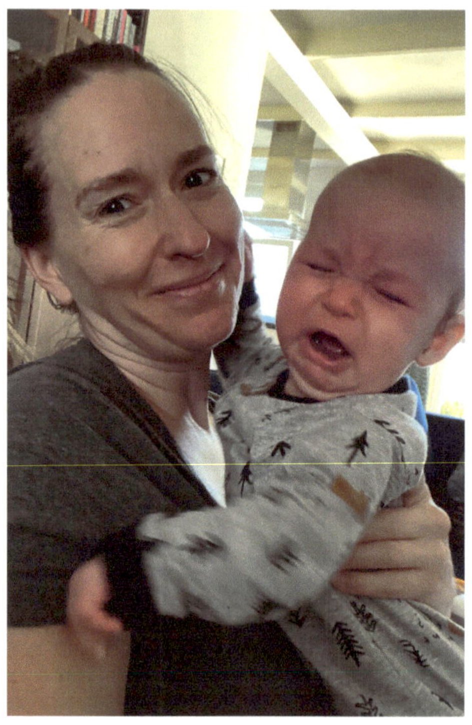

*Inspired by my son Leo,
with gratitude for the support of my partner Maarten.*

Milk art journal
Vol. 1 - Chores & Transcendence
March 2023

Publisher
House of Oktober
houseofoktober.com

Editor
Katherine Oktober Matthews

Contributing artists
Reut Asimini, Colleen Barry, Talia Chetrit,
Kate Falvey, Rachael Grad, C.S. Griffel,
Emma Hardy, Csilla Klenyánszki,
Sarah Lightman, Kath Lovett, Julie Phillips,
Sim Chi Yin, Elena Skoreyko Wagner,
Tabitha Soren, Annie Hsiao-Ching Wang,
and Designing Motherhood

Cover image
Mary's Torments of the Passion (NW3)
2022 © Sarah Lightman
sarahlightman.com

Concept & Design
Katherine Oktober Matthews
oktobernight.com

This book has been typeset in
Utile Display, designed by Sibylle Hagmann, and
Edita, designed by Pilar Cano.

ISBN 9789493075023
© 2023 House of Oktober

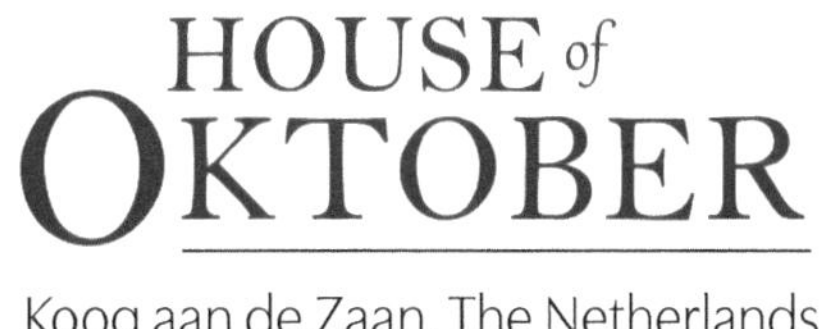

Koog aan de Zaan, The Netherlands